Graciousness

Graciousness

Tempering Truth with Love

John Crotts

Reformation Heritage Books
Grand Rapids, Michigan

Reformation Heritage Books
3070 29th St. SE
Grand Rapids, MI 49512
616-977-0889
orders@heritagebooks.org
www.heritagebooks.org

Printed in the United States of America
26 27 28 29 30 31/10 9 8 7 6 5 4 3

Library of Congress Cataloging-in-Publication Data

Names: Crotts, John, 1968- author.
Title: Graciousness : tempering truth with love / John Crotts.
Description: Grand Rapids, Michigan : Reformation Heritage Books, 2018. | Includes bibliographical references.
Identifiers: LCCN 2017053449 (print) | LCCN 2017053944 (ebook) | ISBN 9781601785879 (epub) | ISBN 9781601785862 (pbk. : alk. paper)
Subjects: LCSH: Courtesy. | Christians—Conduct of life. | Love—Religious aspects—Christianity.
Classification: LCC BJ1533.C9 (ebook) | LCC BJ1533.C9 C76 2018 (print) | DDC 241/.4—dc23
LC record available at https://lccn.loc.gov/2017053449

*Dedicated to my wife, **Lynn**,*
who by God's grace has patiently endured
my growth in graciousness.

Although we met a few years into our Christian lives and after the Lord had already knocked off a few of my rough edges, you have been by my side for many more steps of refinement. May God help us both to be more like our Lord, who was full of grace and truth.

Contents

Preface

The story behind this book about cultivating graciousness in the hearts of those enflamed for God's truth is highly personal. Early in my Christian life, the Lord used biblical debates with Christians from many different theological traditions to sharpen my understanding of the teaching of the Bible and to develop a passion to know and communicate more and more of God's truth. Sadly, in those early days, my sincerity and earnestness were not always coupled with Christlike kindness; in other words, I sometimes used the Bible as a club, leaving fellow Christians battered and bruised.

The Lord has used His truth and many wonderful people to help me grow in graciousness. Serving as the pastor of Faith Bible Church, Sharpsburg, Georgia, for over twenty-two years has provided a precious opportunity to minister God's truth while becoming refined by it. I am grateful to God for the wonderful Christian brothers and sisters in the church whom I have served alongside of throughout these years. Anna Maupin, a church member before Lynn and I arrived, was especially helpful with her early editorial work on this book.

Much of the material forming the content of this book originated from my doctor of ministry program at The

Southern Baptist Theological Seminary in the area of biblical spirituality. The professors Don Whitney, Michael Haykin, and Joe Harrod all helped me with their investments of wonderful lectures, meaningful assignments, and personal time. The program was a shot of spiritual vitality into my long-term pastorate. I especially appreciate Don's personal encouragements and suggestions throughout this work.

I am grateful to Joel Beeke, Jay Collier, and the staff of Reformation Heritage Books for their desire to see the message of this book broadcast to the wider body of Christ. Special thanks goes to Annette Gysen for her excellent editorial work.

My precious wife, Lynn, and our children, Charissa, Danielle, Chloe, and Josiah, have patiently supported their busy husband and dad throughout this book project. I thank God for the grace He has given to our family as we seek to serve Him and love one another, and to have a great time doing both. Thank you for your encouragements, sacrifices, patience, and love. May He help us to excel still more in love.

Chapter 1

Why This Issue Is Important for You

Imagine if you had the opportunity to spend an afternoon with an expert in an area in which you really could use help. Or, what if a famous PGA golfer hits the brakes in front of your house after he notices your tragic efforts at swinging a golf club? He then climbs out of his car with an offer of personal instruction. What if you need a money makeover and Dave Ramsey happens to call you to get together to plan your path to financial freedom?

Now—and I'm just making this up—suppose that when your personal expert finally appears, his breath is awful. As he blows his much-needed wisdom at you, the garlic cloves in your cupboard start to shrivel up and die. Is it possible that this person actually digested a skunk? No matter how good and necessary the content of his conversation, you no longer want to hear it. You need space. You need oxygen. The message may be clear and good for your ears to hear, but your nose wants nothing to do with it.

Sometimes we have some important things to say to our Christian brothers and sisters, but the way we say it directly affects the way they receive our message. Sharing your message with harshness, a critical spirit, a condescending attitude, anger, or even a scowl is like communicating wonderful things with terribly bad breath. The person you are talking to could completely miss out on the benefits of your message simply because of the way you deliver it.

God cares about more than just the words you say. He also cares about how you say those words. It is not enough always to say the truth; you must also say the truth in love. The Lord Jesus Christ provides the greatest model of a person with zeal both to know and to apply the truth of God. Although He knew the truth better than anyone who ever lived, He was never guilty of selfishly showing off His understanding of the Scriptures. While He used the Word of God to correct and admonish others who needed it, His necessary corrections came accompanied with virtues such as love, gentleness, and kindness. These virtues can be summarized as graciousness. The apostle John describes Jesus as "full of grace and truth" (John 1:14). For zealous Christians to faithfully follow their Lord, they must pursue God's truth in their minds and practice, but they must also intentionally cultivate graciousness in their hearts and lives.

The first decades of the twenty-first century have seen a massive revival of the study of the Protestant Reformation's theological teachings. In the late twentieth century, many evangelical pastors and church leaders were drawn primarily to pragmatic conferences and read a diet of devotional and practical Christian titles. Today, however, attendance at Christian conferences, especially those that feature distinctively theological and in-depth biblical messages, has now swelled to the thousands. Publishers are springing up to produce more and more theological and biblical books to satisfy the appetites of hungry readers. The demand for expositional sermons and even Reformed theological lectures online has multiplied, too.[1] This increased appetite for biblical and theological truth among Christians all over the world positively reflects more of the Bible's ideals for Christians and churches. These new attitudes embody the heart of the psalmist, who wrote:

> Blessed is the man
> Who walks not in the counsel of the ungodly,
>   Nor stands in the path of sinners,
>   Nor sits in the seat of the scornful;
> But his delight is in the law of the LORD,
>   And in His law he meditates day and night. (Ps. 1:1–2)

> The law of Your mouth is better to me
> Than thousands of coins of gold and silver....

> How sweet are Your words to my taste,
> Sweeter than honey to my mouth!...

> Therefore I love Your commandments
> More than gold, yes, than fine gold! (Ps. 119:72, 103, 127)

We who value the Bible's importance in Christians' lives rejoice at the new zeal for God's truth throughout the Western world. According to the Bible, zeal for the truth is

---

1. These trends have been traced in John MacArthur, *Ashamed of the Gospel* (Wheaton, Ill.: Crossway, 2010); Colin Hansen, *Young, Restless, and Reformed* (Wheaton, Ill.: Crossway, 2008); Jeremy Walker, *New Calvinism Considered* (Darlington, England: Evangelical Press, 2013); and Mark Oppenheimer, "Evangelicals Find Themselves in the Midst of a Calvinist Revival," *The New York Times,* January 3, 2014, sec. U.S., accessed November 13, 2014, http://www.nytimes.com/2014/01/04/us/a-calvinist -revival-for-evangelicals.html.

a vital part of a faithful Christian's life. God has given His Word to reveal Himself to His creatures, and it is the means by which people see their sinfulness and need for the Savior. God's Word has all that Christians need for life and godliness as they grow with respect to their salvation (2 Tim. 3:15–17; 2 Peter 1:3–4). Is it enough, however, for faithful believers to be merely zealous for God's truth?

The Christian life must be filled with an increasing knowledge and application of biblical truth. Christians who have accurate knowledge of the Bible and theology yet have not thoroughly applied that knowledge to their own hearts, however, may become swollen with pride (1 Cor. 8:1). Many young Christians who discover Reformed theology for the first time enter what has been called the "cage phase." In their first months of being convinced of correct doctrine, these passionate Christians tend to use their new understanding of God's truth to impress, crush, or coerce those around them and should be put into a cage until the phase passes. They are using their newfound knowledge of the truth like a club to assault those around them who have different understandings of the Bible. Although it may have taken these zealous Christians years to understand a point of theology and advocate it as a conviction, they impatiently and aggressively challenge those who delay agreeing with them. In a contemporary expression of Reformation theology, authors Daniel Montgomery and Timothy Paul Jones describe the Bible's teachings about God's sovereignty over man's salvation. They advocate the proper application of these teachings as humility and grace, but they confess that they have been guilty of expressing the truth with more zeal than love. "At times Calvinists—the two of us included—have defended these five points about grace in ways that showed little grace toward fellow believers. And for that, it's time to repent. Calvinism for the sake of Calvinism is not worth fighting for—but grace is always worth fighting for."[2]

Some suppose the antidote to the truth zealots' harsh tones is a lesser love for the truth. Instead of fighting for truth, we should ignore theological distinctiveness and all get along, they advocate. But the truth of the Bible is manifestly so important for the believer's grasp of the identity of the Creator God—His character, His ways, and His will for humanity—that he or she cannot love truth too much. The Lord Jesus Christ proves to be the ideal to which Christians must strive. While Jesus knew God's revealed truth like no other person, He never used God's truth in inappropriate ways. His graciousness always matched His knowledge of the truth.

In 1 Corinthians 13:1–3, Paul uses hyperbole to emphasize the profound importance of Christian love. In three overstated examples, Paul moves from extreme high to extreme low to demonstrate the importance of love:

> Though I speak with the tongues of men and of angels, but have not love, I have become sounding brass or a clanging cymbal. And though I have the gift of prophecy, and understand all mysteries and all knowledge, and though I have all faith, so that I could remove mountains, but have not love, I am nothing. And though I bestow all my goods to feed the poor, and though I give my body to be burned, but have not love, it profits me nothing.

---

2. Daniel Montgomery and Timothy Paul Jones, *PROOF: Finding Freedom through the Intoxicating Joy of Irresistible Grace* (Grand Rapids: Zondervan, 2014), 137.

According to the apostle, a person can fluently speak the language of angels, know all spiritual mysteries, and sacrifice all that they have for others, but if those extreme virtues don't also come with corresponding love, they accomplish nothing, they count for nothing, and that person is nothing. Love is that important to the Lord.

What is the real antidote to the crisis of truth zealots who verbally club people over the heads with their Bibles? The rich contents of the Bible must work through their minds and down into their hearts and lives. In his epistle, James says, "Be doers of the word, and not hearers only, deceiving yourselves" (James 1:22). The Bible tells us about God and His ways—that God is loving and kind and all His followers should be loving and kind as well. Christians must put that truth into action. They cannot love in the ways God wants them to apart from the truth, but they must never try to separate God's truth in their minds from God's love in their lifestyles. The Bible describes the graciousness antidote that zealous Christians are to pursue.

While much has been said in both practical and technical works about the importance of Christians cultivating graciousness, there is a notable absence of practical instructions for Christians to work out this grace in their lives. The purpose of this book is to address that issue.

The faithful Christian life cannot be lived merely with zeal for truth but must also cultivate corresponding graciousness. This book will describe graciousness biblically and demonstrate its essential place in the hearts of faithful Christians. Doing so will involve the study of positive examples and commands about graciousness as well as the negative consequences for those who lack grace. Also included in this book is a wide variety of practical methods for cultivating graciousness in the Christian life. This will equip Christians who are passionately committed to truth to put on a corresponding Christlike heart of graciousness.

Chapter 2

The Graciousness You Need

Different people can believe the same truth from the Bible but express that truth in different ways, resulting in different responses in their hearers. Evan is convinced that the church meets on the Lord's Day to reach unbelievers with the gospel, but Rick believes that the church gathers for believers to worship God and build one another up in the Lord, and unbelievers are only welcome guests. As these two sincere Christians run into one another at the local coffee shop, they exchange perspectives. Tensions begin to rise as the conversation continues. Both Evan and Rick support their points of view from the Bible. Rick, however, becomes heated as he makes his case to Evan, not only motivated by his conviction that the Bible is true but also because he believes that he is giving the more biblical position. Rick's voice becomes strident, and he starts to mock those who believe like Evan, comparing Evan's views to a shallow celebrity preacher. Rick assumes he is completely right, impatiently finishing Evan's sentences and beginning to retort before he really understands Evan's concerns.

Rick's conclusions may be correct, but his manner undoes his message. Later in this chapter we will drop by the coffee shop to watch another friend join the conversation and convey the same perspective as Rick, but with kindness. The seasoning of grace is a catalyst to an edifying conversation.

Although God uses His truth to change the minds and hearts of His people, He works through means. Every person God uses to express His truth is flawed. But according to God's design, adding graciousness to communication produces added persuasiveness. The inspired authors of the Scriptures teach the importance of using graciousness throughout their writings (e.g., Eph. 4:15, 29). The pure word of God is designed to be delivered by people so gripped by God's grace that they express that truth even to their opponents with tact and kindness.

God spoke through King Solomon with great clarity about the importance of graciousness in a person's speech. Solomon gave his instruction using contrasting parallelism, which is a device of Hebrew poetry. He depicts the sweet fruit of graciousness in complete contrast with the destruction of a harsh mouth:

> A gracious woman retains honor,
> But ruthless men retain riches.
> The merciful man does good for his own soul,
> But he who is cruel troubles his own flesh.
>   (Prov. 11:16–17)

> The thoughts of the wicked are an abomination to
>   the LORD,
> But the words of the pure are pleasant. (Prov. 15:26)

Other proverbs simply make the positive case for grace:

The heart of the wise teaches his mouth,
And adds learning to his lips.
Pleasant words are like a honeycomb,
Sweetness to the soul and health to the bones.
    (Prov. 16:23–24)

He who loves purity of heart
And has grace on his lips,
The king will be his friend. (Prov. 22:11)

In order for a person to know what direction to go, he or she must clearly identify the destination. This chapter will define graciousness and its biblically parallel ideas like gentleness, kindness, and love by considering how the terms are used in key texts of the Scriptures. What exactly is gracious speech? Gracious speech is words and tones marked by pleasantness, kindness, the will to help, to encourage, and to convey regard. It is pleasantness; it is being kind; it is having a desire to help and to be a blessing to another person.[1] Clifford Pond explains, "Graciousness is an absence of deliberate aggravation and any kind of rabble-rousing; it is impregnated with courtesy, love, humility, and transparent sincerity."[2] Such speech is not being harsh, critical, or judgmental. Pond adds, "A gracious speaker always has the good of others at heart and not their hurt."[3] As David Hubbard notes in his commentary on Proverbs, "Kind words from a respected person are a

---

1. David Allan Hubbard, *Proverbs* (Nashville, Tenn.: Thomas Nelson, 1989), 225.

2. Clifford Pond, *The Beauty of Jesus* (London: Evangelical Press, 1994), 33.

3. Pond, *Beauty of Jesus*, 33.

prescription for incredible effectiveness."[4] Graciousness is the right medicine for all kinds of maladies of the heart.

Sometimes Christians must say hard things, such as when they must rebuke and correct a stubborn friend or warn a false teacher. These words need to be clear and firm—they will not always be encased with pleasantness. As Christian lawyer and mediator Ken Sande observes, "Of course, there are times when you must speak to others in a firm or even blunt manner, especially if they have refused to pay attention to a gentle approach and are persisting in sinful behavior. Even so, it is wise to take a gentle approach first and get firmer only as necessary (1 Thess. 5:14–15)."[5] There is also a place for righteous indignation against those who have hardened themselves into heresy and hypocrisy. To those in danger of being drawn away from the truth, the prophets, the apostles, and the Lord Himself would sometimes burst forth with a passionate warning.[6] And yet there can still be a gracious intent within even a firm rebuke. Rebukes are given in order to help a person in sin or to halt someone heading down a foolish path, not to harm the one being rebuked. A person nearby will raise an alarmed voice to alert someone carelessly stumbling forward into a busy street. Such communication may be strong and clear as the voice volume elevates and the tone sparks with urgency. But what is the motive behind the mouth in such situations? Is it to be harsh and critical, or is it to rescue a friend from danger? Solomon asserts, "Faithful are the wounds of a friend"

---

4. Hubbard, *Proverbs*, 224.

5. Ken Sande, *The Peacemaker: A Biblical Guide to Resolving Personal Conflict*, 3rd ed. (Grand Rapids: Baker, 2004), 171.

6. David Bailey, *Speaking the Truth in Love: Life and Legacy of Roger Nicole* (Birmingham, Ala.: Solid Ground Christian Books, 2006), 189.

(Prov. 27:6). Christian communication must never be self-motivated but marked by graciously building up other people based on their needs (Eph. 4:29). While there are times Christians must speak with firm directness, usually they should begin with sweetness. On the related virtue of gentleness, Paul Tripp comments, "Gentleness means I don't damage the very person I am seeking to help. Gentleness doesn't mean compromising the truth. Rather, it means keeping the truth from being compromised by harshness and insensitivity."[7]

While descriptions such as Tripp's seem simple, there is depth and breadth to the Bible's teachings about graciousness. Cultivating graciousness requires a patient pursuit of the profound implications of the way the Bible unfolds the concepts.

The Depth of Graciousness

Jesus described the pipeline that exists between a person's heart and mouth. As Jesus exposed the Pharisees, who spoke bad words in bad ways because their hearts were bad, He declared, "Brood of vipers! How can you, being evil, speak good things? For out of the abundance of the heart the mouth speaks. A good man out of the good treasure of his heart brings forth good things, and an evil man out of the evil treasure brings forth evil things" (Matt. 12:34–35). Another time Jesus taught His disciples the place of outward actions and the priority of the roots of a person's heart condition: "But those things which proceed out of the mouth come from the heart, and they defile a man. For out of the heart proceed evil thoughts, murders, adulteries, fornications, thefts, false

---

7. Paul David Tripp, *War of Words: Getting to the Heart of Your Communication Struggles* (Phillipsburg, N.J.: P&R, 2001), 189.

witness, blasphemies. These are the things which defile a man, but to eat with unwashed hands does not defile a man" (Matt. 15:18–20). In addition to words that can be gracious or harsh, tone of voice, facial expressions, and other nonverbal messages originate from the heart of the communicator.

In the biblical concept of anatomy, the heart is the center of a person's inner self. It is where he or she thinks, feels, develops attitudes, and makes decisions. The heart is the fountainhead of a person's true self, which explains Solomon's strong admonition, "Keep your heart with all diligence, for out of it spring the issues of life" (Prov. 4:23). We have already seen the direct connection between the heart and the mouth in Proverbs 16:23: "The heart of the wise teaches his mouth, and adds learning to his lips." A heart-level source lies behind every outward manifestation of either graciousness or harshness.

The Breadth of Graciousness

Surveying four key passages in the New Testament will strengthen our grasp of the breadth and significance of biblical graciousness. In addition to using the term "graciousness," the Bible uses parallel ideas of love, kindness, gentleness, and patience. These qualities overlap and blend together to produce the godlike virtues that God calls His children to manifest in their dealings with each other and with the rest of the world.

Graciousness Humbly Seeks to Strengthen Others

In 1 Corinthians, Paul answers a series of questions the Corinthians had asked him. The phrase "now concerning," which appears several times in the second half of the letter, introduces these questions that Paul addresses. The issue of food being offered to idols is the question Paul addresses in chapter 8, but he answers in such a way that he instructs the church about the larger issue of loving Christians who have consciences easily offended by certain matters. He says, "Now concerning things offered to idols: We know that we all have knowledge. Knowledge puffs up, but love edifies" (v. 1).

The specific knowledge to which Paul refers is the theological truth that idols aren't real gods; therefore, eating food offered to idols is a nonissue. Paul affirms that theological knowledge is a good and necessary acquisition for all believers. But in this specific case, some members of the Corinthian church had large amounts of theological knowledge dangerously divorced from loving practice. They used their knowledge to harmfully cause some of their fellow church members to stumble into sin. Instead of letting their theological knowledge flow through their hearts into loving actions, they became filled with pride.

Israel's Dead Sea is the lowest spot on planet Earth. It receives input from the Jordan River, meager amounts of annual rainfall, and streams that provide small seasonal offerings, but the Dead Sea has no outlet. Water and minerals flow in, but they do not flow out, and they stagnate into a chemically toxic situation for anything trying to live below the surface. Likewise, people with great zeal to take in and understand God's truth who do not then work that truth out in their character and within loving relationships will develop a stagnation of spiritually toxic pride and ultimately spiritual death.

According to Paul, love uses theology to build up other Christians. If biblical knowledge is compared to an instruction manual for assembling a project, a man could foolishly devour the manual in order to become a mere theoretical scholar of building things. Such a person could pounce on others who had different ideas about putting together projects. Citing exact page numbers, he could even quote the manual in the original Chinese language in which it was written. While his head became inflated with facts, he missed the entire point of the manual. In this illustration, the manual exists for the actions of building the project; in the case of true Christianity, love uses theological knowledge to build up the spiritual character of fellow Christians.

The same idea of building up fellow Christians appears in other places in the New Testament. Later in the letter to the Corinthians, Paul mentions building up the church by means of spiritual gifts. The Holy Spirit has given each Christian gifts and abilities to strengthen others in the church. A symptom of pride within the Corinthian church was the people's desire to use their spiritual gifts to show off or to build themselves up spiritually. Paul exhorts them, on the other hand, to use their gifts in ways that build up others in the body of Christ (1 Cor. 14:1–5, 17–19, 30–33). In another letter Paul tells the Ephesians that all of a Christian's words should be uttered in ways to build up others in the church family: "Let no corrupt word proceed out of your mouth, but what is good for necessary edification, that it may impart grace to the hearers" (Eph. 4:29). The Bible's standard for speech is incredibly high. Every word that comes across a Christian's lips must be infused with grace in order to build up the people who hear. There are no vacations or even coffee breaks permitted in order to unleash harsh, critical, unkind, or harmful speech—a believer's mouth must always be on duty, speaking good words in good ways at the right time.

Graciousness Accompanies Truth in Mutual
Ministry among Christians

The apostle Paul lays out the Lord's comprehensive strategy for churches to bring themselves to maturity in Ephesians 4:11–16:

> And He Himself gave some to be apostles, some prophets, some evangelists, and some pastors and teachers, for the equipping of the saints for the work of ministry, for the edifying of the body of Christ, till we all come to the unity of the faith and of the knowledge of the Son of God, to a perfect man, to the measure of the stature of the fullness of Christ; that we should no longer be children, tossed to and fro and carried about with every wind of doctrine, by the trickery of men, in the cunning craftiness of deceitful plotting, but, speaking the truth in love, may grow up in all things into Him who is the head—Christ—from whom the whole body, joined and knit together by what every joint supplies, according to the effective working by which every part does its share, causes growth of the body for the edifying of itself in love.

The Lord Jesus first gives gifted men to His churches (the church leadership). Their task is to equip the members of the church to minister to one another. As the whole church family serves each other, a stabilizing maturity develops—the church is less susceptible to the cunning and craftiness of false teachers. The major means of ministry given to the church for this equipping and ministering is the Word of God. But a critical component of the comprehensive strategy is that the Word must be communicated to others in a particular manner: "But, speaking the truth *in* love, [we] may grow up in all things into Him who is the head—Christ" (Eph. 4:15, emphasis added). Notice several observations about this sentence.

The word "but" shows that Christians serve each other in a different way from the false teachers. Dangerous people will come with destabilizing crafty schemes and will intentionally try to lure vulnerable church members away from the truth. In order to counteract these influences, true believers are to verbalize God's truth to one another.[8] As believers draw near and interact, each one's spiritual needs will become apparent. At different times Christians need different things. Some need encouragement while parenting a rebellious teenager, others need a rebuke because they are willfully sinning, others need wisdom about a job change, some need comfort at the loss of a friend, and others may need to understand more of what the Bible teaches about the person of Jesus Christ. The Bible has everything Christians need for life and godliness (2 Peter 1:3–4). Christians receive this biblical help as fellow church members communicate it personally during times of specific need. There is no craftiness or scheming to undermine the other Christian. Instead, fellow believers express and apply God's truth to give strength and support to the one in need.

---

8. Cf. John R. W. Stott, *The Message of Ephesians*, The Bible Speaks Today (Leicester, England: Inter-Varsity Press, 1986), 171–72. Stott interprets the participle "speaking the truth" as "truthing," understanding it to be more comprehensive—Christians both speaking and living God's truth in love. But the term is used of verbal testimony, and in this context it is in direct contrast to the verbal contents of the false teachers. See P. T. O'Brien, *The Letter to the Ephesians*, The Pillar New Testament Commentary (Grand Rapids: Eerdmans, 1999), 310–12.

Another contrast with the false teachers in Ephesians 4 is the motivation for the teaching. The false teachers desired to deceive those they spoke to. God's truth, however, must be ministered in love. The confession of Christian truth can be cold and unattractive if unaccompanied by the spirit of Christian love.[9] Love seeks the welfare of the person being addressed. Frank Thielman writes, "Love involves seeking the benefit of the undeserving, even at one's own expense…and is bound up with humility, gentleness, and a willingness to work together for unity and peace (Eph. 4:2–3)."[10] Love appears as a lofty theme in this entire letter to the Ephesians. Love motivated God to choose a people for Himself before time began (1:4–5). Love motivated God to raise spiritually dead rebels to life and give them saving faith (2:4–5). Paul prays for the Ephesian church to be spiritually strong enough to be able to grasp the amazing love of Christ for them (3:17–19). He includes love, alongside lowliness, gentleness, and longsuffering, as vital ingredients in maintaining Christian unity within the church (4:2–3). Christian husbands are to love their wives after the self-sacrificial love of Jesus Christ for His church (5:25).

The goal of this truth-and-love ministry is comprehensive growth in Christ. The Lord Jesus Christ is the perfect Head or ruler of His body (Eph. 1:22–23), but like a human baby with an oversized head and an undersized body, the body of Christ must grow to match its Head. Each part of Christ's body has

---

9. F. F. Bruce, *The Epistle to the Colossians, to Philemon, and to the Ephesians,* New International Commentary on the New Testament (Grand Rapids: Eerdmans, 1984), 352.

10. Frank Thielman, *Ephesians,* Baker Exegetical Commentary on the New Testament (Grand Rapids: Baker, 2010), 285.

a part to play in ministering God's truth in godly ways to see Christ's maturity goals for His people accomplished.

Graciousness Evidences Trusting God to Change Others
In his final letter in Scripture, Paul instructs Timothy to persevere in Christian ministry. As Paul nears his death, his priorities for his protégé rise to the surface. Timothy must be a man of God's inspired and profitable word—learning it, holding on to it, and passing it on to others in private and public ministry. It would not be enough merely to hold to the truth in a cold and calculated manner, however. Timothy was to live out the grace of the Lord that is revealed in that true word.

Theological controversies often breed quarrels. Paul repeats the dangers of participating in theological wrestling matches throughout the Pastoral Epistles to Timothy and Titus (e.g., 1 Tim. 1:3–7; 4:1–5; 6:2–5; Titus 3:9–11). While Timothy is to fight the good fight and hold to the truth with an iron-strong grip when it is being attacked (1 Tim. 6:12; 2 Tim. 4:7), he must not be drawn into speculative debates, which often move beyond the bounds of the Bible. These are most likely to produce quarrels. Even when holding firm to the truth, fighting the opponents is not allowed: "But avoid foolish and ignorant disputes, knowing that they generate strife. And a servant of the Lord must not quarrel but be gentle to all, able to teach, patient, in humility correcting those who are in opposition, if God perhaps will grant them repentance, so that they may know the truth, and that they may come to their senses and escape the snare of the devil, having been taken captive by him to do his will" (2 Tim. 2:23–26).

The root term translated "strife" and "quarrel" in verses 23–24 was used in the ancient world to refer to fighting with weapons, but it was used in the New Testament for nonphysical wars of words, in which one person set out to verbally destroy his opponent (2 Cor. 7:5; Titus 3:9; James 4:1).[11] Paul had already told Timothy that an elder must not be characterized by this kind of fighting spirit (1 Tim. 3:3). Here, in the context of theological fighting, Paul reiterates its prohibition. Instead of seeking to destroy the theological enemy, the servant of the Lord Jesus is to be kind to everyone.

The minister is not to hurl invectives at his opponent but is to offer instructions. He must clearly seek to communicate the truth. Paul's mention of patience and enduring evil implies that these gentle instructions might not be received well by the other person right away. His or her response to the gracious efforts of the instructor may lack kindness and gentleness, but Paul calls Timothy to bear up under such without resentment.

A gracious heart exuding kind and gentle manners can accomplish correction. Teaching can be both positive and negative. An elder, according to Paul, must know God's truth well enough to positively exhort God's people in sound doctrine, and to negatively rebuke those who contradict that truth (Titus 1:9). Timothy must take a stand on God's truth in order to gently instruct others faithfully but also to correct those who are teaching against that truth.

The phrase "in humility" is emphasized by its forward position in the sentence in the original language.[12] This term adds to gentleness notes of humility, courtesy, consideration,

---

11. John A. Kitchen, *The Pastoral Epistles for Pastors* (The Woodlands, Tex.: Kress Christian Publications, 2009), 383.
12. Kitchen, *Pastoral Epistles for Pastors*, 384.

and meekness. It is the opposite of brashness, haughtiness, and rudeness.[13] This gentleness is part of the fruit that the Holy Spirit produces in God's children (Gal. 5:23). Gentleness is also an essential virtue when seeking to rescue a brother or sister caught up in any kind of trespass: "Brethren, if a man is overtaken in any trespass, you who are spiritual restore such a one in a spirit of gentleness, considering yourself lest you also be tempted" (Gal. 6:1).

Pragmatists justify using a harsh, aggressive, firm, and often loud tone of voice when they deal with those who disagree with them. They rationalize that their harshness lets their opponent know how serious they are about their point of view. Such contests can be won because of intimidation and submission rather than because the other person is persuaded of the disputed truth claims. Pragmatists would not want to remove harshness from their cache of weapons. But true change doesn't come through brutal tones and language. According to 2 Timothy 2:25–26, it is always God who changes hearts and minds. These opponents need to repent and come to the knowledge of the truth. For those who do not understand the truth, there is a moral and intellectual component that must be addressed, but it is not the intensity of the argument that will yield the desired effect. God causes change. He uses His truth graciously conveyed to create a different heart direction within the opponent. This change should always be the desired outcome, rather than the pride of having won a battle and leaving an opponent flattened and humiliated in the dust. Because the outcome is always in the

---

13. John R. W. Stott, *The Message of 2 Timothy: Guard the Gospel*, The Bible Speaks Today (Downers Grove, Ill.: InterVarsity, 1984), 78.

hands of God, His methodology can be used with confidence. God works through the means of His Word being clearly, patiently, and gently taught.

Graciousness Creates Gospel Openings with Unbelievers
Believers are to show consistent kindness in their communication with fellow Christians, but they are also to speak kindly to unbelievers as a means of opening up doors for the gospel message to be proclaimed. Paul eagerly asked the Colossian church to remember him in their prayers. His main concern was for opportunities to share the gospel and clarity of speech when they came: "Continue earnestly in prayer, being vigilant in it with thanksgiving; meanwhile praying also for us, that God would open to us a door for the word, to speak the mystery of Christ, for which I am also in chains, that I may make it manifest, as I ought to speak" (Col. 4:2–4).

While Paul was an apostle engaged in frontline evangelism, requiring a steady supply of prayer support, he gave the Colossians the task of being part of the process of evangelism as well: "Walk in wisdom toward those who are outside, redeeming the time. Let your speech always be with grace, seasoned with salt, that you may know how you ought to answer each one" (Col. 4:5–6). Having gracious speech was part of what they were called to do. Notice that the context, however, is still about sharing the gospel with outsiders. As Christians go about their daily work in the world, they are to walk wisely. Their heads are to be up; their eyes are to be open. Because the time of every life is limited, Christians need to take advantage of opportunities to prepare other people for the life to come. Seeking these opportunities in the world takes both wisdom and grace. As believers interact with outsiders to the faith, they are called to relate to them graciously as God has related graciously to them. Earlier in the letter, Paul had mentioned his prayers of thanksgiving for those in the Colossian church who had believed the gospel of Jesus Christ, "which has come to you, as it has also in all the world, and is bringing forth fruit, as it is also among you since the day you heard and knew the grace of God in truth" (Col. 1:6). The Christians in Colossae had heard about God graciously offering to forgive their sins through the person and work of the Lord Jesus and had experienced the fruit of their faith developing in their lives, so gospel grace became the platform of engagement with all those around them in their town who had not yet trusted in Christ.

The Colossians' gracious speech was to be seasoned with salt. As food becomes more appetizing when proper seasonings are applied, so also gracious conversations create positive interest and opportunities for deeper explanations of the gospel sources of the sweetness.

The Lord has dealt kindly with His people, and He calls them to emulate His example in their dealings with fellow believers as well as with outsiders. Gracious speech begins in the heart. It is loving, pleasant, and kind, seeking the welfare of the person to whom it is directed. It uses God's truth to strengthen the character of others. When someone strays from the truth, God rescues and restores that person as others come and speak God's truth gently. Sometimes clear corrective words must be used, and even rebukes. But the motivation for strong speech should not be to win an argument, to be critical of others in order to elevate oneself, or even to seek revenge on someone who takes a different view. The motive of God's people speaking graciously is love, based on the love that

God has shown to His people through the gospel of the Lord Jesus Christ.

The Coffee Conversation Revisited

As Christopher ordered his coffee, he noticed his friends Evan and Rick engaged in an intense discussion about something in the Bible. As he approached them, he realized the debate related to the goal of the gathered church—does the church meet for believers or unbelievers? Christopher's entrance functioned like a time-out, giving Evan and Rick a chance to catch their breath and settle their hearts. When the discussion resumed, Christopher weighed in. Like Rick, Christopher understood that the church gathers for believers to worship God and build each other up, and unbelievers are welcome guests. He even used some of the same arguments as Rick but without Rick's argumentative style. Rick sat still, watching Christopher choose to be gracious in his tone and choice of words. Christopher patiently listened to Evan's point of view and then respectfully challenged Evan to consider other truths from Scripture and their implications. Although Evan didn't decide to change churches that day, he genuinely listened to Christopher's perspective. Because Evan realized that Christopher had considered his point of view, his heart was opened to Christopher's kind approach.

If Evan did change his understanding of the primary purpose of the gathered church, it would not have been because Christopher was nice. God uses His truth to change the hearts of others. Christopher's graciousness, however, was the conduit God used to convey his conviction to Evan. Just as God graciously revealed His truth to rebellious, unworthy creatures, He expects His truth to be spread through gracious men and women. While the story of Rick, Christopher, and Evan is only an illustration of biblical graciousness, the Bible provides true examples of graciousness in action, the greatest of which is Jesus. We'll learn from His gracious example in the next chapter.

Chapter 3

Learning from the Gracious Example of Jesus Christ

God made people to imitate others. Long before they enter a classroom, children learn to use complex language and grammar correctly by imitating those around them. Solomon wisely warned his son to pay careful attention to those he spent time with because of the power of their example for good or bad: "He who walks with wise men will be wise, but the companion of fools will be destroyed" (Prov. 13:20). In order to expand our understanding of the Bible's teaching about graciousness, let's consider some examples. The ultimate example of every virtue is the Lord Jesus Christ. Although He is fully God and fully man, He lived on the earth as a man filled with the Holy Spirit. He lived perfectly to fulfill all righteousness and to qualify to die on the cross in the place of guilty sinners, but He also lived perfectly among us to give us the ultimate example of how to live. Included in his model life was a pattern of graciousness in His dealings with others.

The Incarnation

Jesus's graciousness began to be revealed even before He came to earth to be born of Mary. The very act of choosing to come to our fallen world was most gracious. Paul commends Jesus's gracious attitude as something for all Christians to emulate. He describes Christ as the one "who, being in the form of God, did not consider it robbery to be equal with God, but made Himself of no reputation, taking the form of a bond-servant, and coming in the likeness of men" (Phil. 2:6–7). In 2 Corinthians 8:9, Paul depicts Jesus as the ultimate example of giving: "For you know the grace of our Lord Jesus Christ, that though He was rich, yet for your sakes He became poor, that you through His poverty might become rich." His journey of giving from the extreme riches of preincarnate glory to the extreme poverty of living among us and dying on the cross is summarized by Paul as "the grace of our Lord Jesus Christ."

His Actions

The Lord Jesus's gracious heart manifested itself time and again in His activities during His earthly ministry. Heart-level grace is demonstrated in kind words and actions that seek the welfare of the people being engaged. Certainly the perfect Son of God could have scornfully condemned the moral filth spewing from every person He met. Even if He did choose to meet some unworthy person's need, He might have done so in a cold, calculated manner, just dutifully demonstrating His deity. Jesus did not do anything like that. His actions modeled kindness, compassion, gentleness, and patience—in other words, graciousness.

The Gospels consistently depict Jesus as feeling compassion for the needy people around Him. The common term translated "compassion" literally means "bowels," the inner place where a person feels warm, deep sympathy for someone else.

Jesus felt compassion for the Jewish people, who were harassed and helpless sheep without a shepherd, and prayed for them (Matt. 9:36). He felt such sympathy for the needs of the crowds that He ignored His own needs, teaching them God's word and healing those who were diseased (Matt. 14:14; Mark 6:34). When the multitudes stayed with Jesus for three days to hear His teaching and had nothing to eat, He felt compassion for them and fed them (Matt. 15:32). He even broke up the funeral of a widow's only son because He felt compassion for the widow and raised her son from the dead (Luke 7:13–15).

The term for compassion is not used of Christ in the account of the rich young ruler; rather, "love" is used. After this man confidently asserted that he had kept all God's commandments from his youth, Jesus looked at him and loved him (Mark 10:21). Consider what Jesus did not do at this point in the story: He did not critically correct the egotism of this young man. He could have rattled off the man's sins like a machine gun, shattering his arrogance into a million pieces. Jesus did expose the man's covetousness by calling him to sell his possessions and give to the poor, but His words did not come from a heart of harshness. Jesus loved this young ruler and put before him the prospect of treasure in heaven and a relationship with Him.

The Lord Jesus also displayed His graciousness by the company He chose to keep. He ministered to women and welcomed children and sinners to Himself, something that was not done by the self-respecting religious leaders of that day. Jewish rabbis didn't speak to women in public, especially not Samaritan women, but Jesus intentionally put Himself in Samaria by a well when a woman came to draw water. John 4 recounts the surprising conversation that followed. Jesus graciously helped her see her sin and her need for eternal life through Him. He met the needs of many other women as well. In John 8, instead of condemning the guilty woman caught in adultery, Jesus mercifully called her to repentance.

While in New Testament times Jewish and Roman families loved their own children, society did not value children as a whole. So when some people sought to approach Jesus to lay His hands on their children and offer a blessing, His disciples intervened. "But Jesus said, 'Let the little children come to Me, and do not forbid them; for of such is the kingdom of heaven.' And He laid His hands on them and departed from there" (Matt. 19:14–15). What kind of man must Jesus have been to take up little children in His arms and pray for God's special blessing on them? Theologically speaking, these depraved children were born in sin and already deserved God's wrath in Adam's fall (Ps. 51:5; Rom. 5:12–21). Did Jesus scowl with disgust as the sinful babies were brought near? Did His eyes flash with divine judgment? The disciples would not have had to work so hard to keep children away from a stern man. Instead, the Lord Jesus graciously received these children and held them up as an illustration of receiving the kingdom by dependent faith in Him. While the disciples sought to keep children away from Jesus, religious leaders sought to keep Jesus away from notorious sinners, like prostitutes and tax collectors. Far from worrying about His reputation, Jesus literally ate and drank with them and ministered to their needs. He was called a "friend of tax collectors and sinners" (Matt. 11:19).

The disciples of Jesus, who were often marked by a slowness to understand and believe, experienced the graciousness of Jesus many times. Although Jesus regularly pointed out their little faith and small understanding, He did not expel them from His school; instead, He patiently cared for them with further instruction and more opportunities to make spiritual progress. The nineteenth-century Anglican bishop of Liverpool, J. C. Ryle, described the Lord's dealings with His disciples as "nothing but unchanging pity, compassion, kindness, gentleness, patience, longsuffering, and love. He does not cast them off for their stupidity. He does not reject them for their unbelief…. He teaches them as they are able to bear. He leads them on step by step, as a nurse does an infant when it first begins to walk."[1]

His Teaching

The Lord Jesus Christ preached what He practiced. His tender dealings with those in need around Him matched His words of instruction and invitation. While the worst of men and women can love people who love them, Jesus shocked His followers by calling them to love those who could not return the favor: "But love your enemies, do good, and lend, hoping for nothing in return; and your reward will be great, and you will be sons of the Most High. For He is kind to the unthankful and evil. Therefore be merciful, just as your Father also is merciful" (Luke 6:35–36). Meeting the needs of undeserving people is one of the most godlike things a person can do. Jesus holds up His Father as the standard of mercy for His people to strive after. A man's pride allows him to show kindness only to those he deems worthy, but if his pride is great enough, no

---

1. J. C. Ryle, *Holiness: Its Nature, Hindrances, Difficulties, and Roots* (Moscow, Idaho: Charles Nolan Publishing, 2001), 251.

one but him will ever qualify. Such a proud heart produces attitudes, words, and actions across a spectrum that includes indifference, disdain, criticism, impatience, and cruelty. Jesus, however, replaces pride with mercy.

When Jesus encountered the flint-like hardness of heart of the people in the cities where He had done many of His miracles during His Galilean ministry, He turned to God the Father in prayer. After rejoicing in God's sovereign grace that had opened the eyes of some people, Jesus issued this sweet invitation: "Come to Me, all you who labor and are heavy laden, and I will give you rest. Take My yoke upon you and learn from Me, for I am gentle and lowly in heart, and you will find rest for your souls. For My yoke is easy and My burden is light" (Matt. 11:28–30). As the Lord opened the doors widely for burdened sinners to find forgiveness through Him, He also revealed His gracious character. Unlike the Pharisees, who crushed the people of Israel with their exacting demands regarding the Mosaic laws, their tedious traditions, and meticulous Midrash, Jesus was gracious with an easy yoke to bear. He promised rest for the weary.

His Character

Seven hundred years before the Lord Jesus came to earth, the prophet Isaiah predicted that the Messiah would be God's special servant. His prophecies about the servant include descriptions of graciousness that Jesus perfectly fulfilled. Matthew wrote his gospel with particular sensitivity to a Jewish audience, pointing out many of these Jewish prophecies from the Old Testament that Jesus fulfilled. After Jesus withdrew from the religious leaders' opposition, avoiding capture because it was not yet His time to die, He healed many people in need. Matthew recalled Isaiah 42 in his analysis of the event:

> That it might be fulfilled which was spoken by Isaiah the prophet, saying:
>
> > "Behold! My Servant whom I have chosen,
> > My Beloved in whom My soul is well pleased!
> > I will put My Spirit upon Him,
> > And He will declare justice to the Gentiles.
> > He will not quarrel nor cry out,
> > Nor will anyone hear His voice in the streets.
> > A bruised reed He will not break,
> > And smoking flax He will not quench,
> > Till He sends forth justice to victory;
> > And in His name Gentiles will trust."
> > (Matt. 12:17–21)

Jesus lived out this messianic mission prophesied by Isaiah. The weak and needy—the "smoking flax"—did not find a Christ who blasted their failures, but one who gently sought to keep their tiny spark kindled. Writing about the Holy Spirit's influence on Jesus in His earthly mission, Sinclair Ferguson notes:

> Here we find reference to his meek and gracious spirit in the pursuit of righteousness. He does not break the bruised reed or quench the dimly burning wick; he does not draw attention to himself or parade his own abilities. This is the consequence of the divine gift, "I will put my Spirit on him" (Is. 42:1). What Paul will describe as "walking in the Spirit" and bearing "the fruit of the Spirit" (Gal. 5:22–26) finds its prototype in Jesus himself, as does Paul's

rich description of love as the first and most essential mark of the Spirit (1 Cor. 13:1ff.).[2]

At the Cross

Nowhere is Jesus's graciousness more fully displayed than in His suffering and death on the cross. Peter uses the example of Jesus enduring the cross to show church members how they ought to respond to unjust suffering.

> Servants, be submissive to your masters with all fear, not only to the good and gentle, but also to the harsh. For this is commendable, if because of conscience toward God one endures grief, suffering wrongfully. For what credit is it if, when you are beaten for your faults, you take it patiently? But when you do good and suffer, if you take it patiently, this is commendable before God. For to this you were called, because Christ also suffered for us, leaving us an example, that you should follow His steps:
>
> "Who committed no sin,
>
> Nor was deceit found in His mouth";
> who, when He was reviled, did not revile in return; when He suffered, He did not threaten, but committed Himself to Him who judges righteously.
> (1 Peter 2:18–23)

Karen Jobes notes that in this section of his letter, "Peter points to the slave, who was the most vulnerable in Greco-Roman society, as a paradigm for the Christian believer who

2. Sinclair B. Ferguson, *The Holy Spirit* (Downers Grove, Ill.: IVP Academic, 1997), 52.

follows Jesus Christ."[3] God intentionally calls His people to endure persecution such as this and makes submission to unjust masters possible by His grace. When God calls believers to suffer in this way, He commends a kind, merciful response, because those are the characteristics of the response Jesus made to those unjustly accusing Him and ultimately executing Him. Christians can be gracious in such extreme circumstances by having their consciences tuned toward God (v. 19), just like Jesus, who "committed Himself to Him who judges righteously" (v. 23). Thinking about God's sovereignty, wisdom, providential outworking of His greater plan, and faithfulness enables us to have quiet hearts and offer gracious replies when we suffer undeserved abusive treatment. To underscore his point, Peter specifies the ungracious, sinful things that Jesus did not say on the cross. He uttered no sinful slanders, deceitful retorts, or bitter threats. He did not suggest the possibility of unleashing an army of angels or even warn those attacking Him that God would be bringing their false accusations up at the judgment.[4]

The Gospels record sayings that Jesus uttered with great effort during the time He suffered asphyxiation on the cross. Each of Jesus's seven sayings provide insight into His heart as He endured agonizing hours of physical, emotional, and even spiritual torture. In spite of such a massive trial, Jesus

---

3. Karen H. Jobes, *1 Peter*, Baker Exegetical Commentary on the New Testament (Grand Rapids: Baker Academic, 2005), 180.

4. When facing unjust charges, Paul, in contrast to Jesus, actually did threaten God's judgment to the high priest in Acts 23:3: "Then Paul said to him, 'God will strike you, you whitewashed wall! For you sit to judge me according to the law, and do you command me to be struck contrary to the law?'"

maintained graciousness. He was nailed to the cross; He felt the shock as it was dropped into a hole in the ground; He was shamefully placed between a pair of convicted criminals. But Jesus said, "Father, forgive them, for they do not know what they do" (Luke 23:34). This unjust, cruel punishment cried for justice. The innocent victim, the Lord Jesus Christ, prayed for mercy instead.

The crowds were inspired by the Jewish leaders and the Roman soldiers to mock those being crucified, especially the Man in the middle. Amazingly, the criminals on both sides of Jesus joined in the jesting. After some time, one of the criminals felt remorse, repented, and went on to rebuke his partner in crime. Luke recorded the sequence:

> Then one of the criminals who were hanged blasphemed Him, saying, "If You are the Christ, save Yourself and us."
>
> But the other, answering, rebuked him, saying, "Do you not even fear God, seeing you are under the same condemnation? And we indeed justly, for we receive the due reward of our deeds; but this Man has done nothing wrong." (23:39–41)

The penitent thief then turned to Jesus and asked that Jesus would remember him when He came into His kingdom. Jesus's gracious reply to this undeserving man, who was guilty as charged of his crimes and who had initially participated in mocking Him, was, "Assuredly, I say to you, today you will be with Me in Paradise" (Luke 23:43). While dying for the sins of all who would believe in Him, including this thief, Jesus graciously met the man's deepest need for mercy.

When Jesus Did Not Seem Gracious

Although Jesus lived a life full of grace and truth, an honest Bible reader must recognize the few times in Jesus's earthly ministry when He did not seem gracious. Would that temple money changer have thought that the Lord Jesus was being nice and gentle when He trashed his tables and scattered all over the ground the money the man had been profitably exchanging? What about all the others in the temple that day who had turned God's house of prayer for the nations into a den of robbers (Matt. 21:12–13; cf. John 2:12–14)? If people from Capernaum or Bethsaida or Chorazin (Matt. 11:20–24) were in the crowd, how might they have heard Jesus's denouncements of their cities? Jesus said about Capernaum, "And you, Capernaum, who are exalted to heaven, will be brought down to Hades; for if the mighty works which were done in you had been done in Sodom, it would have remained until this day. But I say to you that it shall be more tolerable for the land of Sodom in the day of judgment than for you" (Matt. 11:23–24). Could an unfavorable comparison to Sodom ever count as graciousness? At the dinner table, would the Pharisee tell his wife and children that Jesus was kind as he described the devastating series of woes Jesus pronounced against the Pharisees and the scribes in Matthew 23?

The guilty individuals whom Jesus addressed in these situations might not have experienced His graciousness in the way that a child Jesus tenderly embraced would have, but we need to give careful thought to these special examples before we judge Jesus to be sinfully ungracious. In these incidents in His ministry, Jesus was not simply reacting in the way that a person might react to a difficult situation. In other words, the Lord Jesus wasn't just having a bad day, so He decided to take it out on the money changers in the temple. He wasn't merely frustrated with a few random Pharisees who believed differently from Him as He cursed them to hell. His condemning comments about the Galilean cities do not draw a parallel with a harsh review someone might post on a website after a bad experience in another city.

In these examples from His ministry, Jesus was straightforward and direct, and He strongly threatened His listeners of God's judgment. After much gracious revelation to the nation and its leaders, the Lord Jesus finally made pronouncements of judgment toward those who repeatedly rejected the message He brought as the Messiah of Israel. At this final hour, however, Jesus still had gracious intentions even as He gave His strongest indictments. But even though most of the people Jesus was addressing did not recognize His graciousness, many individual Pharisees and first-century Jews did respond to Him, repenting and believing in Him. A good shepherd cares for his sheep by eliminating the wolves, so others benefited as Jesus exposed and judged evil influencers. Millions of people who have read the inspired record of these events in the Bible have also bowed the knee before King Jesus as He revealed Himself in grace and in His pronouncements of judgment.

The Lord Jesus was concerned for God's glory and for the good of the people He spoke to and those whom they influenced. It may not initially seem gracious when a doctor pulls up a sick woman's sleeve and pierces her skin with a sharp needle to inject medicine or when he uses a razor to cut through the patient's skin to remove a cancerous tumor. The effects of needles and razors can be quite painful, but in the hands of a skillful doctor they are instruments of ultimate healing. The doctor does not inflict pain against his patients as retaliation for feeling offended; he is doing what is necessary for their ultimate good. Sometimes the doctor graciously cares for a community by removing a sick person so contagious that he requires being quarantined. With His strong words, Jesus had the godly intention of inflicting pain in order to bring about healing and life.

While a father's or mother's discipline can be harsh and angry, which is always sinful, God's Word assumes that all loving fathers and mothers should rightly discipline their children. According to the author of Hebrews, human fathers and the heavenly Father discipline their children out of love and for their ultimate good:

> Furthermore, we have had human fathers who corrected us, and we paid them respect. Shall we not much more readily be in subjection to the Father of spirits and live? For they indeed for a few days chastened us as seemed best to them, but He for our profit, that we may be partakers of His holiness. Now no chastening seems to be joyful for the present, but painful; nevertheless, afterward it yields the peaceable fruit of righteousness to those who have been trained by it. (12:9–11)

Discipline is painful rather than joyful. But should we think of discipline rightly performed as harsh, critical, judgmental, or unkind—all categories that are the opposite of graciousness? Absolutely not. Exercising discipline is motivated by love for the one being disciplined: "For whom the LORD loves He chastens, and scourges every son whom He receives" (Heb. 12:6). We could think of discipline as short-term pain a parent inflicts lovingly, motivated by a desire to do a child long-term good; God exercises discipline so that His children will share His holiness. We could compare Jesus's stern speech to the believing but wayward among the Jews to the stern words of a father to his child.

Although fallen human beings' motives are often tainted by hidden sins and selfishness, Jesus's motives never were. Jesus exhibited righteous anger a few times in His ministry, but it is difficult to discern righteous anger in those with deceitful hearts (Heb. 3:13). When Jesus communicated intensely with others, He was never sinfully angry; rather, He was motivated by defending and declaring the glory of God. When Jesus was personally attacked, He was gracious, even when He was reviled on the cross, but when God's glory or His divine purposes in His mission as Messiah were at stake, He answered boldly.[5]

The Lord Jesus Christ is a wonderful priest to His people. He represents His people before God, and through His righteous life, sacrificial work on the cross, and intercessory ministry He provides access to God for all who trust Him. Because the Lord lived among us, He sympathizes with our weaknesses, and He deals even more gently with His people than a sinful priest ever could (Heb. 4:15; 5:2). He is a loving, kind, and gentle shepherd. Although He never compromises on God's Word, which reveals God's glory, He is gracious to His imperfect followers. He is the greatest model of graciousness anyone could ever follow. Because of remaining sin, however, even redeemed human beings will never attain the

---

5. John MacArthur, 2 *Timothy*, MacArthur New Testament Commentary Series (Chicago: Moody, 1995), 99–100.

standard of grace that Jesus set. Thankfully, in the Bible are intermediate mentors of graciousness who sought to follow Christ's perfect example and thus became examples for Christians. One of those wonderful examples of a harsh person turned gracious, by God's grace, is the apostle Paul, whom we will consider in the next chapter.

Chapter 4

Learning from Paul

While the Lord Jesus Christ never gave in to the temptation to be sinfully harsh, the same cannot be said for Saul of Tarsus, who is better known to Christians as the apostle Paul. According to Paul's testimony, he fully imbibed the strict pharisaical Judaism in which he was raised. Therefore, when Jesus's ministry began overturning the Jewish system of laws and traditions, Paul became enraged. His zeal for what he thought God wanted led him to vent fury against Jews who had turned to Jesus. He stood by in a position of approving oversight and assistance, holding the garments of those who stoned Stephen, the preacher of the Lord Jesus (Acts 7:58; 8:1). After that pivotal event, Paul's rage intensified. The first church historian, Luke, recounted that "as for Saul, he made havoc of the church, entering every house, and dragging off men and women, committing them to prison" (Acts 8:3).

Paul's Intensity before Coming to Christ

As the persecution developed, Paul was deputized by the chief priests of Israel to expand his mission of cruelty to Christians: "Then Saul, still breathing threats and murder against the disciples of the Lord, went to the high priest and asked letters from him to the synagogues of Damascus, so that if he found any who were of the Way, whether men or women, he might bring them bound to Jerusalem" (Acts 9:1–2). Elsewhere in Scripture, Paul described his actions during this time: he was binding men and women, imprisoning and beating those who believed in the Lord; casting the death vote against Christians; persecuting the church violently and trying to destroy it; and was a blasphemer, persecutor, and insolent opponent (Acts 22:4; 26:10; 1 Tim. 1:13). He says of himself, "And I punished them often in every synagogue and compelled them to blaspheme; and being exceedingly enraged against them, I persecuted them even to foreign cities" (Acts 26:11). Even after he repented and trusted in Christ, his reputation so preceded him that Christians were afraid to take him in. When the Lord told Ananias to go see Paul and baptize him, Ananias felt compelled to remind the Lord about Paul: "Lord, I have heard from many about this man, how much harm he has done to Your saints in Jerusalem. And here he has authority from the chief priests to bind all who call on Your name" (Acts 9:13–14). When people heard Paul in the Jewish synagogues, they were amazed and asked, "Is this not he who destroyed those who called on this name in Jerusalem, and has come here for that purpose, so that he might bring them bound to the chief priests?" (Acts 9:21). Not until Barnabas confirmed Paul's conversion did Christians in Jerusalem overcome their fear and meet the man (Acts 9:26–28).

When people are converted to Christ, they are made new, but not completely new. They are declared righteous before God, are indwelt by the Holy Spirit, and are given new desires and abilities to please the Lord (Phil. 2:12–13; 3:8–10). But throughout their lifetime, they will progress in putting off their old sinful attitudes and ways of the flesh and in putting on the new spiritual ways of the Lord (2 Cor. 3:18; Gal. 5:16–18). On the trip to Damascus, when Paul, furious with zeal, was leading a team to persecute more followers of Christ, the Lord Jesus appeared to him and changed his direction. Paul repented of his sin and believed in Jesus. This conversion marked the rest of Paul's life. His raging anger toward Jesus and His followers melted into grace. The mercy of the Lord toward such an awful, unworthy opponent affected Paul to the core of his being and would be worked out throughout the rest of his life.

Paul's Inconsistency after Coming to Christ

After his conversion Paul's temper would flare at times, and he would lash out against other people as he had previously. He had an intense disagreement with Barnabas over John Mark, and, as previously mentioned, he threatened the chief priest with the judgment of God when he was on trial unjustly (Acts 15:36–40; 23:3). The Bible does not tell us everything about such occasions, so we must be cautious about reading things into the material that is recorded. The Lord Jesus Christ never crossed the line into sinful anger; His concerns were always God's glory and the good of those to whom He spoke. On the other hand, Paul, like the rest of sinful humanity, sometimes failed to be gracious. But undoubtedly a viciously angry man can be transformed by the grace of God more and more into a gracious man. This is the hopeful, encouraging example of the apostle Paul.

Examples of Paul's Kind Ministry

Paul's gracious example shines through in his dealings with churches and individuals. Following the four Gospels, the book of Acts gives the inspired record of the early church. The rest of the New Testament is comprised of letters to churches, groups of Christians, and individual Christians, followed by the book of Revelation. Paul authored thirteen of these inspired letters. Within his sacred mail we see glimpses of the historical occasion for the letters and the caring heart of the one who sent them.

Of the churches that Paul founded, he had the least personal experience with the church at Thessalonica. Although the book of Acts describes Paul's team working in the city on only three Sabbaths, which culminated in a hasty escape to Berea, there are clues in his two letters to that church that Paul had ministered there at least a few months. His first letter to the Thessalonians is perhaps Paul's most personal. He seeks to encourage them to continue on in the Lord in spite of the persecutions they were experiencing. He encourages them to grow even more in their love for one another and corrects misunderstandings about the coming of the Lord. But Paul also had to counteract some people who were calling into question his character and ministry. While Paul did not make it a habit to defend his reputation for its own sake, the fact that he was sent from the Lord Himself and established that church on the Lord's gospel meant that defending his ministry in this case was actually a defense of the word of God. His motivations for ministry were not about greed or glory but were marked instead by graciousness and sacrifice.

Paul writes to the Thessalonian believers, "But we were gentle among you, just as a nursing mother cherishes her own children. So, affectionately longing for you, we were well pleased to impart to you not only the gospel of God, but also our own lives, because you had become dear to us" (1 Thess. 2:7–8). Paul compares his relationship with these young believers to a mother gently caring for her children. A newborn baby is utterly dependent on its mother for care and nourishment, so God gives mothers a special tenderness, which they use in caring for their fragile little ones. Paul loved the young church; he communicated with them tenderly for their benefit. He wasn't selfishly sharp with them; instead, he gave them his very self—motivated by his sincere affection for them. The term translated "gentle" here is the same word Paul used in 2 Timothy 2:24 about the kind way a minister must handle opponents: "A servant of the Lord must not quarrel but be gentle to all." This attitude of kindness must mark ministers of the Lord's truth as they serve everyone, from the youngest Christians to those who directly oppose the minister's understanding of the truth.

Certainly Paul also needed to be straightforward with the young Thessalonian church from time to time. This plain talk, however, was not born out of a heart of bitterness or impatience. Rather, Paul compared his strongest engagements with this church to a father and his children: "You are witnesses, and God also, how devoutly and justly and blamelessly we behaved ourselves among you who believe; as you know how we exhorted, and comforted, and charged every one of you, as a father does his own children, that you would walk worthy of God who calls you into His own kingdom and glory" (1 Thess. 2:10–12).

Unlike Paul's brief interactions that characterized his relationship with the church in Thessalonica, years of personal experience shaped his relationship with the church in Corinth. But in both situations, Paul's reputation, which was directly connected to the gospel and the foundation it provided for the instruction Paul gave the churches, was being attacked and required a defense. By the time of his second letter to the Corinthians, Paul had to defend himself boldly. If false apostles and their false message were going after the hearts and minds of the church he founded, he needed to intervene in every way that he could. He wasn't ashamed to beg. The tone of the final three chapters in 2 Corinthians shifts remarkably from the first nine chapters. He had to make his point. He had to win back their confidence, not to him personally as much as to the message of Christ that he had proclaimed. As strong, clear, and even aggressive as he would be, he begins these closing chapters with these sweet words: "Now I, Paul, myself am pleading with you by the meekness and gentleness of Christ" (2 Cor. 10:1). Paul's goal was to emulate the Lord Jesus's gracious attitudes and actions. Even though he would be bold when God's glory or God's word was at stake, as in his public opposition to Peter when that apostle's actions contradicted the gospel (Gal. 2:11–14) and later in this letter to the Corinthians, Paul was mindful of Christ's grace to him and wanted to interact with even wayward Christians with entreaties that reflected the Lord's grace. Grace-inspired love was the goal of all his instruction everywhere he went (1 Tim. 1:5).

A final example of Paul's graciousness is the letter he wrote to Philemon. Philemon was a leader in the church at Colossae. When Onesimus, Philemon's runaway slave, found Paul in Rome, Paul introduced the slave to Jesus, and he was converted. Paul's desire was to reunite his new friend Onesimus with his old friend Philemon, so he sent Onesimus back to Colossae with a letter in hand. The letter to Philemon is a model of gracious appeal. Instead of Paul pulling apostolic rank and demanding that Philemon forgive Onesimus's sins and financial debts and even send him back to serve Paul in his Roman house arrest, Paul appealed to Philemon again and again: "Therefore, though I might be very bold in Christ to command you what is fitting, *yet for love's sake* I rather *appeal* to you—being such a one as Paul, the aged, and now also a prisoner of Jesus Christ—I appeal to you for my son Onesimus, whom I have begotten while in my chains" (Philemon 8–10, emphasis added). Later, after offering to pay for any debts Onesimus had incurred, Paul continued to appeal,

> Yes, brother, *let me have joy from you in the Lord; refresh my heart in the Lord.*
>
> Having confidence in your obedience, I write to you, knowing that you will do even more than I say. But, meanwhile, also prepare a guest room for me, for I trust that through your prayers I shall be granted to you. (Philemon 20–22, emphasis added)

Paul's gracious communication in Christ was followed by the hope that Christ would graciously take Paul from captivity in Rome to Colossae, to Philemon's guest room. Coming from an apostle of Christ, these appeals carried a great deal of weight. But it must not be overlooked that Paul did not use his position in a cavalier, arrogant, or authoritative manner. He treated his Christian friend with kindness for Christ's sake. The Holy Spirit superintended all these circumstances and included Paul's inspired letter within the pages of sacred Scripture as a model of the graciousness all believers should emulate.

Chapter 5

The Truth about an Ungracious Church

The Ephesian church may have been the most truth-loving church in the Bible. You might even say they were the original truth zealots. Paul taught in the city of Ephesus for three years—longer than in any of the other cities where he stayed. Some of his ministry in Ephesus is described in Acts 19—speaking boldly in the synagogue, equipping the disciples in the hall of Tyrannus, and apparently launching church planters, because, during his time in Ephesus, "all who dwelt in Asia heard the word of the Lord Jesus, both Jews and Greeks" (Acts 19:10). While in this verse "Asia" refers to the region that surrounded Ephesus, sometimes called Asia Minor, which is found in modern western Turkey, this is a remarkable accomplishment. Luke, the author of Acts, summarized Paul's time there by stating, "The word of the Lord grew mightily and prevailed" (Acts 19:20).

The next chapter of Luke's chronicle recounts Paul's meeting with the Ephesian church's leaders. Their appetite for God's truth is revealed even in the way Paul addresses them. He said that these church leaders knew "how [he] kept back nothing that was helpful, but proclaimed it to [them], and taught [them] publicly and from house to house, testifying to Jews, and also to Greeks, repentance toward God and faith toward our Lord Jesus Christ" (Acts 20:20–21). Paul told them everything that was profitable—"For I have not shunned to declare to you the whole counsel of God" (Acts 20:27). He then charged the elders:

> Therefore take heed to yourselves and to all the flock, among which the Holy Spirit has made you overseers, to shepherd the church of God which He purchased with His own blood. For I know this, that after my departure savage wolves will come in among you, not sparing the flock. Also from among yourselves men will rise up, speaking perverse things, to draw away the disciples after themselves. Therefore watch, and remember that for three years I did not cease to warn everyone night and day with tears. (Acts 20:28–31)

This was a church with trained and equipped elders. They knew the truth, they loved the truth, and they were on guard for their lives and their teaching. Their spiritual radar was on high alert for any distortions of the truth. They even received an inspired letter from Paul, which was recognized to be part of the New Testament Scriptures. Paul's letter grounded the church even more firmly in the gospel from eternity past to the full inclusion of the Gentiles in the salvation promises to Israel. Paul spent the second half of the letter to the Ephesians working out the implications of the gospel in daily living in the church, at home, and in the frontlines of spiritual battles.

Later, in Paul's first and second letters to Timothy, we find that Timothy was left in Ephesus. Paul reiterates his mission in that city for Timothy's sake, but probably for the Ephesians' sake as well: "As I urged you when I went into Macedonia,"

Paul begins, "remain in Ephesus that you may charge some that they teach no other doctrine" (1 Tim. 1:3). The Pastoral Epistles passionately emphasize the truth: know the truth, preach the truth, live the truth, breathe the truth, guard the truth, entrust the truth to others, and watch out for anybody teaching anything different from the truth. Church ministry done God's way is all about the truth. The church at Ephesus received their passion for the Scriptures from Paul for several years and then from his right-hand man, Timothy, for many more years. Apparently, the Ephesian church got the message about the importance of truth.

A Church Lacking Love

Revelation 2 and 3 record letters from Jesus to seven first-century churches. These letters offer many wonderful insights into what Jesus approves of and disapproves of in churches that actually existed. Everyone today can find a little bit of each of these first-century churches in their church—Jesus's words are relevant. The first letter is addressed to the church in the biggest city in that part of the world, Ephesus—the truth-loving church we have been considering.

Our Lord Jesus begins His letter to this church by commending the Ephesians for their love for the truth. Can you imagine the feeling that would sweep over you if Jesus personally applauded your passion for His truth? He did just that for these believers. In Revelation 2:2, Jesus says, "I know your works, your labor, your patience, and that you cannot bear those who are evil. And you have tested those who say they are apostles and are not, and have found them liars." Later in the letter Jesus adds, "But this you have, that you hate the deeds of the Nicolaitans, which I also hate" (Rev. 2:6).

The Nicolaitans, about whom little is known, were false teachers. They show up again in Jesus's letter to the church at Pergamum. In Revelation 2:15–16, Jesus says, "Thus you also have those who hold the doctrine of the Nicolaitans, which thing I hate. Repent, or else I will come to you quickly and will fight against them with the sword of My mouth." Previously in that letter, Jesus condemns the teaching of Balaam, who caused God's people to stumble through sexual immorality and eating food sacrificed to idols. Those errors may be related to the Nicolaitan teaching. The point for this discussion is the Nicolaitan teaching was against Scripture. The Ephesians loved the truth; therefore, they hated the false teaching of the Nicolaitans. Note as well that Jesus encouraged the Ephesians by telling them that He also hated the false teaching of the Nicolaitans. Christians in a politically correct culture, where few people draw sharp moral lines, must hear the Lord Jesus saying, "I hate the teaching of the Nicolaitans." The truth is more important than many Christians today believe. The Ephesian church is commended for hating false teaching, opposing it, and removing those falsely claiming to be apostles.

We cannot read Jesus's letter to the truth-loving Ephesians, however, and come away encouraged on their behalf. Loving people is also more important than many Christians today think. After Jesus's commendations, there is an ominous word, "nevertheless": "Nevertheless I have this against you, that you have left your first love. Remember therefore from where you have fallen; repent and do the first works, or else I will come to you quickly and remove your lampstand from its place—unless you repent" (Rev. 2:4–5).

While the "first love" that church left refers to their love for the Lord, the Lord's charge must also concern their love for other people. The Ephesian believers were truth lovers who were harsh. Their love for the truth brought out an edge in the way they dealt with others, probably without and especially within the church. The sharp sword of God was rightly being used to cut the truth from error, but it seems that they were using it to cut each other up as well. Jesus charges them to return to *the works* they had done at first, which refers to loving, good works toward those around them. That is an important reason why this charge seems to refer to their first love for other people and not just their love for the Lord.

A Church Full of Grace and Truth

Why does the Ephesian church case study show us the importance of loving people? In spite of their truth-loving track record on full display before Jesus's eyes, He tells them to repent. They were not ambiguous about their theology or the doctrinal content of those who taught within their church gatherings. The Lord Jesus highly commended these things about the church, but He did not minimize their sinfulness in this situation either. He follows the call to repentance with a strong warning—if the church did not repent, He would come and remove their lampstand. Revelation 1:20 reveals that the lampstands represent the churches. Churches are the Lord's lights shining out in the dark world. Jesus is saying it would be better to have no church in the massive, thriving city of Ephesus than to have an *unloving* church, even if it preaches the truth and opposes people who oppose the truth. Being gracious in the way we speak truth to others forms a vital part of what Jesus requires from His people. We might think Jesus would be accommodating to a church committed to so many right things. He is not. He says that He is going to personally come and snuff out their candle. Their church would be eliminated; it would not shine out in Ephesus any longer. Speaking God's truth in a loving and gracious way is that important.

A beautiful new sports car parked in front of a crowded restaurant grabs the attention of many people who eat there or walk anywhere close to it. Silent admiration and longings bubble up into all kinds of excited exclamations. Many spectators would be tempted to compare the beautiful machine before them to their adequate but less impressive vehicle. But what if the hood of the sports car suddenly opened up to reveal an empty shell? The engine and everything else are completely absent. After the initial surprise wears off, spectators might make a different comparison between the sports car that cannot move without a tow truck and their own vehicles, but this time with completely different results. Without the guts of the sports car, it cannot even be called a car. In the same way, a church may look like a church on the surface, even being passionately committed to God's truth, but if it has no love for people, it cannot rightly be called a church. The Lord Jesus said love is such a vital part of a church that He would eliminate such loveless churches from existence if they do not repent.

Chapter 6

Cultivating Graciousness in Your Heart

In a child's art class, the teacher leads the students from theory to practice. At the beginning of the section on the Impressionists, for example, the teacher describes the characteristics of Impressionism, highlighting examples of the best paintings. Then the teacher sparks the children's imaginations with stories of some of the artists. As they "travel" around Paris in the nineteenth century, discovering the backgrounds of men like Pierre-Auguste Renoir and Claude Monet, their understanding of the works of art broadens. Finally, paper and colorful paints are set on their desks. The students are challenged to imitate the masters of Impressionism.

While Christians must depend on the Holy Spirit to effect change in their lives, clearly God expects them also to put forth disciplined efforts to grow in godliness using the means the Holy Spirit has provided (1 Tim. 4:7–8). To this point, this book has considered the importance of graciousness for truth zealots by examining its biblical meaning and by studying real-life examples in action. Now the study becomes practical. Just as the paper and paints are at last placed before the students, the manifold ways truth-loving Christians can cultivate graciousness in their lives will be placed before us for our consideration. Let's begin with the thoughts and attitudes of our hearts. Then we will move on to the words and actions that flow from our gracious hearts.

Rooting Out Harshness

Before a man tries on a new sports coat, he should remove the one he is wearing. Similarly, the Bible compares spiritual growth to changing clothes. Paul charges the Ephesians "that you put off, concerning your former conduct, the old man which grows corrupt according to the deceitful lusts, and be renewed in the spirit of your mind, and that you put on the new man which was created according to God, in true righteousness and holiness" (Eph. 4:22–24). Before believers can put on the virtue of graciousness, they must begin by taking off the vice of harshness. There are several components of rooting out harshness. While some overlap among these components is inevitable, Christians must thoroughly eradicate their wrong ways of communicating in order to cultivate kindness.

Identify the Source of All Speech

Why do people use harsh words, tones, and facial expressions? People don't think carefully about their harshness and offer several common excuses for it, such as foul weather, a difficult day at work or with children at home, physical ailments, and the humorous summary justification of a "bad hair day." Factors such as these may explain some of the circumstances surrounding angry verbal eruptions, but they do not address the true source of the problem. Like doctors striving to cure the problem and not merely treat the symptoms, Christians desiring to root out harshness must locate the source of the problem.

The source of harsh speech is a harsh heart. All speech comes out of the heart. In the anatomy of the Bible, the heart is the control center of a person, where he or she thinks, feels, and makes decisions. The Lord Jesus says in Matthew 12:34, "Brood of vipers! How can you, being evil, speak good things? For out of the abundance of the heart the mouth speaks." Wise King Solomon advises his son, "Keep your heart with all diligence, for out of it spring the issues of life" (Prov. 4:23). Guarding the heart is urgent, because the heart is the headwaters of a person's entire life.

Although the Lord has renewed the hearts of Christians, they have remaining sin inside them. They are not, however, ruled by that sin. The bondage to sin has been broken, but remaining sin continues, and what is in the heart will come out of the mouth. Why is a person ultimately harsh or critical, according to the Bible? While external triggers are situational factors, ultimately the source of harshness is inside the person's heart. Stray sparks do little damage without fuel, but if a spark lands on gunpowder, a great explosion will occur. The gunpowder that has been stored up in the heart reacts to a difficult day with the kids. Without the gunpowder, the external trigger harmlessly passes by undetected. In order to begin to put off harshness, people must cut through the situations of their life and examine the sins of their mind, will, and emotions.

Realize the Evil of Ungraciousness
The beginning of repentance is the sight of sin. In other words, people must see their own sin in its ugliness before they turn

from it in their hearts and lifestyles. Puritan Thomas Watson soberly observed, "A man must first recognize and consider what his sin is, and know the plague of his heart before he can be duly humbled for it…. The eye is made both for seeing and weeping. Sin must be first seen before it can be wept for."[1] Recognizing that the heart of a harsh speech problem is the human heart is a good beginning. Now we must consider the sorts of things contained within a harsh heart. In other words, what kinds of heart thoughts and attitudes form the chemical components of that gunpowder from which ungraciousness explodes? Far deeper and darker are the sources of sin than the sinful words and tones themselves. A person's recognition of the special ugliness of his or her source sins is a first step in repentance and change. Consider some of the possibilities.

Anger. What is it that gives words their attacking edge? Why was there a sarcastic twist on that answer? One possibility is anger toward another individual. Anger in the heart finds its way out through the mouth in ungracious speech.

Manipulation. Sinfully strong words and tones can be used to make a point and win an argument, commandeering the entire discussion. When two people disagree about the Scriptures, one of them, whether right or wrong about the interpretation of a Bible passage, can still "win" by intimidation. The Lord Jesus does not smile at His children who sin to win.

Revenge. Some people use harsh communication to make the other person feel bad for something he or she has said or

---

1. Thomas Watson, *The Doctrine of Repentance* (Edinburgh: Banner of Truth Trust, 1988), 18–19.

done. Determination to hurt someone back says, "I'm going to use my strong tone, my loud volume, and my angry words to punish you and to get back at you." The Bible clearly teaches that Christians are never to seek their own revenge, whether physical or verbal: "Beloved, do not avenge yourselves, but rather give place to wrath; for it is written, 'Vengeance is Mine, I will repay,' says the Lord.... Do not be overcome by evil, but overcome evil with good" (Rom. 12:19, 21).

A lack of love and compassion. First Corinthians 13 is the famous love chapter in the Bible. Love's virtues are described as patient and kind, and not arrogant, rude, or irritable. The opposite of loving others is selfishness, or the love of self. So if you hear words funneling out of your mouth that are unkind, ungracious, and condemning, you can know those words are not showing love to the person you are speaking to. You should stop and consider whom you are loving at that moment.

Thoughtlessness. How often does a person react emotionally to a situation instead of responding thoughtfully? If Jim is hurriedly walking to the elevator to get to his meeting on time and Sharon steps in front of him, he may lash out critically against her. While there could be several reasonable explanations for Sharon's action, or even if Sharon was completely at fault for being in the wrong lane of office traffic, Jim did not respond to the situation in a way that was kind to Sharon; he just reacted. Not carefully guarding our hearts but also our tongues causes sinful styles of speaking.

Impatience. Impatience often hides behind harshness. Thoughts like, "He should have grasped the point by now," or "She *deserved* my strong word to help her understand" inspire agitation. Not waiting patiently for someone can be a source of verbal and nonverbal cruelty.

Pride. The mother of every source sin is pride. Those who are being harsh and critical think they are right. In fact, they are *certain* they are right. Fools are filled with pride. "I don't really care about you and what you think," the fool tells himself. "It's my view or no view!" As Proverbs 18:2 puts it, "A fool has no delight in understanding, but in expressing his own heart."

These sins below the surface are not pretty. It is easier for us to be harsh with others when we don't consider the ugly source for our critical edge. Because Christians, however, want to overcome such wickedness, we must go below the surface of our lips into our hearts. We must identify the foul sources of our sinful speech and call them what they are.

Growing Graciousness
Recognize God's Commands
When you love the Lord, you desire to do the things that God wants you to do. God doesn't just think being gracious is incidental for mature Christian living, He clearly commands all Christians to be gracious. True believers are motivated to obey such commands as they recognize them in the Bible. As has been noted, Ephesians 4:29 forbids corrupting words from coming out of our mouths and calls believers to speak only words that build others up according to the need of the moment, giving grace to those who hear. But just after this come verses 30–32: "And do not grieve the Holy Spirit of God, by whom you were sealed for the day of redemption. Let all bitterness, wrath, anger, clamor, and evil speaking be put away from you, with all malice. And be kind to one another,

tenderhearted, forgiving one another, even as God in Christ forgave you."

Bitterness, wrath, anger, clamor, evil speaking, and malice are characteristic of words that qualify as *ungracious* speech. These are forbidden vices that grieve the Holy Spirit. God has a personal concern that His children use their speech in kind and merciful ways and not at all in ways that are harmful: "But love your enemies, do good, and lend, hoping for nothing in return; and your reward will be great, and you will be sons of the Most High. For He is kind to the unthankful and evil. Therefore be merciful, just as your Father also is merciful" (Luke 6:35–36). Being gracious in your interaction with people inside and outside your church family does not mean you have achieved some elite level of Christianity. Graciousness is fundamental. Christians' words are to be God's instruments of grace to others.

Appreciate That God Is Monitoring Your Mouth
Everyone will be judged by his or her words. The Lord Jesus said, "But I say to you that for every idle word men may speak, they will give account of it in the day of judgment. For by your words you will be justified, and by your words you will be condemned" (Matt. 12:36–37). God is not merely a God of generalities, unconcerned about the details of His creatures' lives. He is sovereign over the hairs of every person's head and over the tiniest sparrow falling from a tree in the woods—He is concerned about details. Many harsh, critical words would be filtered if the speaker of them had a greater awareness of God.

The Bible gives many reasons for people to obey God's commands for sexual purity. One of these motives is that God sees in the dark: "For the ways of man are before the eyes of the LORD, and He ponders all his paths" (Prov. 5:21). In the case of communication, if you knew that God was listening to every word that you were saying and was instantaneously aware of the slightest inflections in your voice, and that He would hold you accountable according to the highest standards of His holiness, would you not speak to others with utmost care? Just as the warm waves of the sun's heat come through the earth's atmosphere before reaching the earth's surface, every one of the waves of sound emitting from your mouth passes through God's active awareness, being stored for accountability on judgment day, even before reaching the earthly hearer's ears. God watches with concern every detail of each of His creature's daily interactions. Having a heightened awareness of God's continual attentiveness to your communication causes you to see the seriousness of being gracious and the danger of being rude.

Repent of a Harsh Heart

True repentance begins by seeing sin for what it is, but it doesn't end there. Once you see how deeply the evil roots of harshness are embedded within your heart, you must turn your heart to the Lord. When the Lord Jesus Christ declared His displeasure with the church at Ephesus's lack of love, He did not think it enough for them to know about love or even think sorrowful thoughts about their condition. He did not ask them merely to remember the early days when they used to be loving. He wasn't looking for their possible rationalizations, like all the false teachers they had had to deal with. He commanded the unloving church to *repent*: "Remember therefore from where you have fallen; repent and do the first works, or else I will come to you quickly and remove your lampstand from its place—unless you repent" (Rev. 2:5). Repentance is a mind-set change that leads to a lifestyle change. For the Ephesians, true repentance would result in reengaging with their initial works of love.

Repentance is not a trivial matter; lacking graciousness is not a small issue. Every heart sin originating and sustaining the sinful words and tones coming from a person's mouth must be dealt with. Instead of following the instinct to justify an angry outburst because of outward circumstances (including the actions and attitudes of the other participants in a discussion), Christians desiring to become like Christ must acknowledge their anger, lack of love, and pride. While others committed sins by provoking you, the Lord holds each Christian responsible for his or her sins.

The oft-quoted words of Jesus, "Judge not, that you be not judged" (Matt. 7:1), prohibit hypocritical judging, not all judgments. In just a few verses, Jesus calls His followers to make a judgment when He says, "Hypocrite! First remove the plank from your own eye, and then you will see clearly to remove the speck from your brother's eye" (Matt. 7:5). Instead of allowing your mind to spin with faultfinding in others and excuse making for yourself, Jesus calls you to examine your heart first. Confess the sins you discover to the Lord. Turn from them with the intention of never returning to them again. Seek to replace those vices with corresponding godly virtue. When we repent of sinful roots of harshness, righteous fruits of graciousness begin to appear.

Discover Grace to Be Gracious
When we understand that selfishness and pride are root causes of harshness, is there any hope of turning back the epidemic of unkind communication? Because of remaining sin, even maturing Christians could be repenting of rude speech every day of their lives. The wonderful message of the gospel is that God is gracious to undeserving sinners. Because of the work of Christ, God forgives His children for their lack of grace, and then He melts their hearts and continually forms them into more gracious men and women. His transforming grace works in several ways, perhaps none more important than by giving believers a personal appreciation of the gospel.

Appreciate God's Graciousness
How difficult is it for you to think of reasons that God could be extremely harsh with you? If you are honest and observant you should be able to come up with a list of sins you have committed in your mind or with your mouth or sinful activities you have done over the course of a week that ought to earn a full measure of God's righteous wrath. Now consider the reason why God *has not* acted in justice toward you. The only reason that He did not punish you is that He crushed His Son for the exact sins that you committed during that week.

God did not blast the sinful you into the lake of fire. In fact, God actually responded graciously toward you. Instead of wrath you received blessings. It is so good to meditate deeply about the reality of your amazing relationship with such a God. Hebrews 12:29 reminds even professing believers that "our God is a consuming fire." Reflection upon your own offenses against such a God and on His mercies to you in

Christ Jesus produces powerful waves of thankfulness to God for His repeated abundant grace.

The parable of the prodigal son wonderfully depicts God's gracious heart toward His children. Luke 15:2 discloses that the story was one of three told to religious leaders who were grumbling because Jesus was being so kind to known sinners. The parable is designed to show God's kind affection for such people. The younger son takes his inheritance and wastes it on scandalous living. When famine strikes, the son becomes impoverished and begins to starve. He is brought low enough to tend unclean pigs and even crave their feed. Eventually, he is broken enough to return home to beg his father for food. The father, representing God, would have had every right to vent his wrath on his foolish son. Instead, the father runs to the son, wraps him with a robe, and puts shoes on his calloused feet and a ring of honor on his dirty finger. Beyond all that, he prepares a feast for his son. Christians should consider how God's kind dealings with them are similar.

You must not go a day without purposefully thanking God for the gracious ways He deals with you. Certainly you should be thankful for His initial forgiveness when you first received Christ, but you must also regularly reflect on the days, months, and years since you trusted Christ. The recent sins of heart, hands, and mouth are far worse than those you committed before coming to Christ. The child of God knows more and has experienced more mercy and yet has kept sinning. Has God ever said to you, His child, "Enough!"? Has He ever cast you away, crying out, "No more!"? No, He has not. The reason is because God's entire furious wrath toward you was poured out on Jesus on the cross. When you give thanks to God repeatedly for His grace to you, it is very hard to be harsh with others.

The subtitle to Ken Sande's outstanding book *The Peacemaker* is *A Biblical Guide to Resolving Personal Conflict*. In seeking to resolve conflicts, Sande wisely notes the vital place of graciousness, which he says originates from a continual recognition of the grace we received from God.

> Peacemakers are people who breathe grace to others in the midst of conflict. Since we cannot breathe out what we have not breathed in, this process hinges on our moment-to-moment relationship with God. We must continually "breathe in" God's grace by studying and meditating on his Word, praying to him, thanking him for his mercy and rejoicing in our salvation, worshipping him, partaking of the Lord's Supper, and enjoying the fellowship of other believers. As we are filled with his grace, we can then breathe it out to others by confessing our wrongs, bringing them hope through the gospel, lovingly showing others their faults, forgiving them as God has forgiven us, and manifesting in our words and actions the fruit of the Holy Spirit.... When even one person in a conflict is faithfully breathing out this kind of grace, others will often receive God's grace through us. As they do, they are less likely to be defensive and more inclined to listen to our concerns.[2]

Jesus also illustrates the importance of being gracious out of the overflow of grace personally received. In Matthew 18:21–22, the author provides the occasion for a parable:

---

2. Sande, *Peacemaker: A Biblical Guide*, 170.

Then Peter came to Him and said, "Lord, how often shall my brother sin against me, and I forgive him? Up to seven times?"

Jesus said to him, "I do not say to you, up to seven times, but up to seventy times seven."

Then Jesus tells the story of the unforgiving servant. The king mercifully forgives the debt of the servant who owes him a huge amount of money, but then that same servant throws a fellow servant into debtor's prison until he can repay him a much smaller amount. Everything seems fine until the king finds out what happened. Jesus explains:

> Then his master, after he had called him, said to him, "You wicked servant! I forgave you all that debt because you begged me. Should you not also have had compassion on your fellow servant, just as I had pity on you?" And his master was angry, and delivered him to the torturers until he should pay all that was due to him.
>
> So My heavenly Father also will do to you if each of you, from his heart, does not forgive his brother his trespasses. (Matt. 18:32–35)

The forgiven servant had a legitimate issue with the man who owed him money. It wasn't just imaginary. Jesus said that the amount that was owed was a hundred denarii. Certainly it was far less than the first servant had owed his master, but a denarius was one day's wage—so the total amount was wages from one hundred days of work. Our Lord Jesus, however, clearly expects His followers to treat other people out of the overflow of super-abundant grace that they have received from Him. The forgiven servant should have been gracious and forgiven the man who owed him the money. As you contemplate the cross of Christ, you should be overwhelmed with the oceans of grace you have received from the Lord. Even when others commit pools or even lakes full of sins against you, you should be gracious to them because of those oceans of grace you have received. "Be kind to them," Jesus would say, "not because they deserve it, but because I have been so kind to you."

In his book *Humble Orthodoxy*, which seeks to balance passion for biblical truth with humility and love, Joshua Harris observes, "Genuine orthodoxy—the heart of which is the death of God's Son for undeserving sinners—is the most humbling, human-pride-smashing message in the world. And if we truly know the gospel of grace, it will create in us a heart of humility and grace toward others."[3] Because of the significance of appreciating God's gospel grace in order to cultivate graciousness, you should continually seek after fresh ways to grow in understanding the depth and breadth and height and width of the love of God for sinners. Reading books, listening to sermons, and memorizing targeted verses can all lead you to a more profound appreciation and personalization of the grace of God toward the individual, which will in turn result in a greater ability to breathe out God's grace toward others.

Be Thankful for Everything Else

As you seek to cultivate graciousness in your heart, you should be thankful for everything beyond the cross in your life. James 1:17 says, "Every good gift and every perfect gift is from above, and comes down from the Father of lights, with

---

3. Joshua Harris, *Humble Orthodoxy: Holding the Truth High without Putting People Down* (Colorado Springs: Multnomah, 2013), 30.

whom there is no variation or shadow of turning." God has given His creatures every good thing that they enjoy in life. The right response from creature to Creator is gratitude. Paul reiterates the humbling truth in a question: "And what do you have that you did not receive? Now if you did indeed receive it, why do you boast as if you had not received it?" (1 Cor. 4:7). Being thankful helps keep that perspective in the forefront of your mind.

Saying thanks to the Lord for everything in life provides needed perspective. No one truly has anything to boast about in themselves. During interaction with others, your consistently grateful heart will recognize that harsh, critical heart attitudes are out of place. One of the reasons why people use unkind tones and words in their interactions is they assume they are correct about an issue, whether it involves the Bible, politics, or any practical matter. Having certainty on an opinion tempts a person to move quickly beyond loving dialogue to confident assertions. Being thankful for everything good about life can inject graciousness into the discussion.

Let's suppose Samuel is a potentially ungracious man in a theological controversy. In this case Samuel happens to be right about the biblical subject under discussion. But every element of his being right about that point comes from God, not from Samuel. There is no room for Samuel's heart to be arrogant when he actively acknowledges that God is responsible for every aspect of his understanding of the truth. Samuel's functioning brain, which ably forms the basis of his true opinions, comes from God. His experiences with people and books that have shaped his understanding have all been ordained by God's providence. Even Samuel having the Bible in his own language is no small gift from God. Why can he read and understand it? Is it not the mercy of the Lord? It is the Holy Spirit of God who illuminates his mind to even understand anything about the Bible (1 Cor. 2:14–16). Absolutely none of these things have occurred because Samuel is so great. They are all the mercy of the Lord. Therefore, Samuel should be humbled and filled with gratitude to the Lord, acknowledging His grace. When he speaks to other people, his grateful heart should season his discussion with graciousness.

Recognize That God Is at Work

In every possible situation in which a man or woman could be tempted to be ungracious, God is at work. As John Piper has remarked, "God is always doing 10,000 things in your life, and you may be aware of three of them."[4] Consider the benefits of such recognition in the promotion of graciousness. When a Christian is aware that God is working in a tempting situation, even when it is in specific ways that he or she does not realize, it fosters graciousness in a couple of ways. First, it cultivates humility. While human beings know they are not omniscient, it is good that they acknowledge it periodically. Not knowing all that the Creator is accomplishing in a situation helps to keep the creature humble. As pride fuels harshness, humility drives it away. But, second, it reminds us that there really is more going on in a situation than a person can know about. So even times when people are 100 percent sure that they are right about what they are saying, they ought

---

4. This quote was one of John Piper's most widely spread posts on Twitter in 2012. John Piper, "God Is Always Doing 10,000 Things in Your Life," *Desiring God*, accessed July 29, 2014, http://www.desiringgod.org/articles /every-moment-in-2013-god-will-be-doing-10-000-things-in-your-life.

to consider that God could be working in ways that they do not know about. Thoughts like that encourage confident people to tone the rhetoric down a little bit.

Consider two examples from the Bible. First, remember Job's counselors. While they are often viewed as complete failures as friends, Job's counselors are surprisingly right in much of their counsel. Yet in spite of their accurate ideals, they were unfaithful friends—God clearly declares that at the end of the book (Job 42:7–9). But why were they such bad guys when they said so many good things? The answer is that they hadn't read Job 1 and 2. In the first two chapters of Job, God and the devil are disputing. God asks Satan if he has considered His servant Job and holds Job up before His greatest enemy as an example of faithfulness. When Satan protests that Job is only righteous because of God's blessings, God permits the devil to rip Job's life to pieces in order to prove that Job's faith will not fail. The devil did just that within the boundaries that God established. Job's life disintegrates almost instantly, and then his friends come to sit with him. They mourn with him for a week before they start talking. They say things to Job such as righteousness is better than sin, sin has consequences, and nobody has such a miserable life like Job's. If God were not working in special ways behind the scenes, how much of what they said would have been bad? What made their counsel so foolish and wrong was that they arrogantly assumed that they knew all that was happening. They did not, and, therefore, their mostly accurate words were *completely inappropriate*. They lacked the spiritual big picture; therefore, they discouraged Job instead of encouraging him in the midst of an epic spiritual battle.

The second example from the Bible is from a strange time in Israel's history, the time of the judges. In Judges 14, the future super-strong judge of Israel, Samson, is introduced as an adult. Troubles with the opposite sex would follow this leader throughout his career. Samson's parents didn't know, however, that God was using their son's earliest wicked desires to marry a Philistine girl in order to lead to a mighty victory over the Philistines, who were oppressing Israel at the time. Judges 14:1–4 describes the details, including a behind-the-scenes insight:

> Now Samson went down to Timnah, and saw a woman in Timnah of the daughters of the Philistines. So he went up and told his father and mother, saying, "I have seen a woman in Timnah of the daughters of the Philistines; now therefore, get her for me as a wife."
>
> Then his father and mother said to him, "Is there no woman among the daughters of your brethren, or among all my people, that you must go and get a wife from the uncircumcised Philistines?"
>
> And Samson said to his father, "Get her for me, for she pleases me well."
>
> But his father and mother did not know that it was of the LORD—that He was seeking an occasion to move against the Philistines. For at that time the Philistines had dominion over Israel.

Without considering Samson's or his parents' questionable wisdom or what actions they all took, notice the small detail of background given to the reader: "But his father and mother did not know that it was of the LORD—that He was seeking an occasion to move against the Philistines." God is always at work in every situation. No matter how certain you may be that you are right, you can be helped toward gracious-ness as you humbly realize that God may be doing more than anyone knows.

Biblical counselors Tim Lane and Paul Tripp rightly observe that God is sovereignly working in people's rela-tionships with many more purposes than just each other's enjoyment:

> Remember, your relationships have not been designed by God as vehicles for human happiness but as instruments of redemption. It isn't enough to ask for the character you need to survive the difficulties of life and the weaknesses of the other person. We have been called to minister to the people that God, in his wisdom, has placed in our lives. He wants to use us as instruments of grace in their lives. To live this way takes character.[5]

The single insight that God is working in many more ways than a person can ever know can transform his or her communication about a situation. Instead of indignation flow-ing from pseudo-omniscience, the believer who thinks about God at work responds with gentleness, making much room for the wise dealings of a sovereign God.

Remember That God Changes Hearts

Christian communicators can be gracious confidently because God is the one who produces the results of conversations they have with others. We have seen God's heart-changing sover-eign work in 2 Timothy 2:24–26, which says, "And a servant

---

5. Timothy S. Lane and Paul David Tripp, *Relationships: A Mess Worth Making* (Greensboro, N.C.: New Growth Press, 2006), 110.

of the Lord must not quarrel but be gentle to all, able to teach, patient, in humility correcting those who are in opposition, if *God perhaps will grant them repentance*, so that they may know the truth, and that they may come to their senses and escape the snare of the devil, having been taken captive by him to do his will" (emphasis added). Once, at a summer construction job, my professing-Christian foreman told me that certain construction workers would not ever receive correction if he did not use profanity to make his point. But it is not the corrector's job to *make the other person get the point*. Instead, it is the corrector's job to speak the truth, and to speak it in love. God is always ultimately the one who will make the other person get the point—if they are to get it at all.

The doctrine of God's sovereign hand controlling everything in the universe is not ivory tower theology; it has some very practical applications. God is the one who works change in the hearts of hearers of instruction. In his book *Encouragement: How Words Change Lives*, Gordon Cheng compares God's work in someone else's heart to God's work with farmers in a harvest: "We are planting and watering, but God through his Holy Spirit is giving the growth. Unless God's Holy Spirit opens the heart of the person to hear and receive the message, our words will be useless—no matter how true they are, or how cleverly we express them. We can't reach inside a person and change their heart for them. God's Spirit can. As he does so, the word can take root and grow and lead to changed lives. We are fellow workers with God."[6]

---

6. Gordon Cheng, *Encouragement: How Words Change Lives* (Kingsford, Australia: Matthias Media, 2006), 50.

Another phrase from the Bible strengthens believers to hope in God as they offer correction gently. "Therefore let us, as many as are mature, have this mind; and if in anything you think otherwise, God will reveal even this to you" (Phil. 3:15). The dynamic that God will ultimately reveal right ways of thinking to immature Christians is encouraging to those feeling burdened to fix everyone else. While this in no way excuses Christians from confronting a fellow Christian in sin or even challenging someone to grow in an area of weakness, it does remove the burden of change from the speaker. It is okay to do your best to graciously help your hearer—then leave the results with the Lord. It is not the strength of your voice or the strength of your harsh tone that fixes people. God takes care of it. You can leave the results to Him.

Think about the Ultimate Goal

Consider the goals you are pursuing in your conversations with others. Sometimes you just want to win the point of contention. While you may tell yourself that your motivation is for the other person to have a more accurate view of theology, for example, sometimes it is more about victory. Just as an athlete passionately wants to win the game, some Christians passionately want to win the argument. Another related motive in arguments is to try to look smart in front of the opponent or others who are present. Never minding the potential spiritual dangers of the other person's biblical or theological errors, some ungracious truth zealots just want to be seen advocating right positions. Precious lambs of the Lord have been badly bloodied by theological bruisers on a mission of triumph. The goal of your every conversation ought to be the glory of God, not winning a point: "Therefore, whether you eat or drink, or whatever you do, do all to the glory of God" (1 Cor. 10:31).

When you engage in debating something from the Bible, it ought to be a helpful experience for both parties, even if it becomes intense, like iron sharpening iron. But if the ultimate aim of God's glory is lost upon either participant, the temptation to escalate passions can become too great. One voice is raised. Someone goes for the kill. Even if one side concedes the point in such a conversation, if the process does not please God, what will He think about the outcome? Since God is the one who produces change within others, He wants His people always to speak to one another in ways that honor Him and demonstrate belief that He is in control of all things.

A mind filled with God is the most powerful force for change within a believer's heart. When you apprehend the true character of God, your perspective on life changes dramatically. You become more aware of the sinfulness of sin as the Holy Spirit illuminates the word of God in your mind. You experience sharp conviction as your sinful attitudes and conversations seem to be in the spotlight before the audience of God. As painful as such discoveries may be, obtaining a Godward perspective is where change begins. Depending on the Holy Spirit, you then utilize personal spiritual disciplines, rooting out your harshness and discovering God's grace. The path to spiritual transformation continues as the individual pursues spiritual disciplines which move beyond just themselves and God, and also involve other people.

Chapter 7

Cultivating a Gracious Mind-Set toward Others

A bull does not belong in the aisles of a china shop. The objects' beauty and value are inconsequential to the beast, so the bull will simply do what bulls do. While some bulls may not buck and thrash about rodeo style, no bull will be as delicate and careful as the situation requires. A few of the precious objects may elude the long, pointy horns of the awkward bull, but his lumbering body will smash china, shattering it into pieces. While bulls lack the poise to walk through china shops, most people are capable of looking without destroying—hence the continued existence of china shops. But even so, stores with expensive china on the shelves do require customers to maintain a heightened awareness of their surroundings. No one wants to be compared to the china shop bull.

The least person on earth is made in God's image and is therefore far more precious than the most exquisite piece of china. You must find ways to treat those around you even more carefully than you navigate the china shop. In addition to the individual spiritual disciplines Christians practice that were considered in the last chapter, there are many other helpful ways for God's people to individually cultivate graciousness in their dealings with other people.

Have a Proper Perspective of Other People

A great beginning for Christians seeking to become kind is to have a heightened awareness of the value of the people with whom they interact. People's perspectives of others can dramatically differ from God's evaluation of those special creatures made in His image.

Properly Appraise People's Value

A few years ago I had the opportunity to meet Sonny Perdue, who then was the governor of the state of Georgia. Although the meeting was brief and informal, I was on my best behavior. Usually when people have the opportunity to interact with a man or woman whom they highly respect, they become very thoughtful. Care goes into exactly what they say and the way they say it. Sometimes, though, we do not value others as highly as we ought to. We are not as thoughtful as we should be; our words and tones become careless, spewing wildly like a fire hose pumping at full strength without anyone controlling it. Our tones and words can become more gracious, however, as we begin to value *all* people in the ways the Lord has revealed.

In two different passages in his epistles, the apostle Paul addresses the problem of Christians causing fellow believers to stumble as a result of their example. In both passages, the Bible uses a phrase that reveals the value we should place on other Christians. Paul says in 1 Corinthians 8:11, "And because of your knowledge shall the weak *brother* perish, *for whom Christ died?*" (emphasis added). And in Romans 14:15, in writing about stumbling blocks, Paul uses the same expression—*"the one for whom Christ died."* How precious is the weakest Christian in the body of Christ? What does Jesus think about their value? These weak Christians are as valuable as the blood of the Lord Jesus Christ.

Jesus taught about stumbling blocks and the people who cause them. He said, "Whoever causes one of these little ones who believe in Me to sin"—He is probably not speaking literally of children per se, but of the childlike faith of believers—"it would be better for him if a millstone were hung around his neck, and he were drowned in the depth of the sea" (Matt. 18:6). Notice three things about Jesus's words. First, a millstone was a big, heavy object—it crushed grains while it rolled in a circle on another heavy stone. Second, someone who wore a millstone as a necklace and went for a swim would sink quickly. Third, Jesus says it would be *better* to sink in the sea than to cause one of His children to sin. The reason Jesus makes such an extreme comparison is because people are extremely precious to Him.

Jose is a follower of Jesus but sometimes struggles with being kind when he speaks to others, especially if he considers them to be below his social status. If Jose's heart could recognize how valuable the people around him are, reflecting the perspective of Jesus, he would tend to interact with them with greater concern. The least, weakest little brother or sister in Christ is incredibly precious and valuable to Jesus and should be to Jose as well. Appreciating the value of others will immediately affect Jose's tones and word choices. When we talk with a fellow Christian, we should realize we are talking to a very important person and adjust our actions accordingly.

On the other hand, what if the person is not a Christian? Could Jose then justify raising his voice, speaking harshly, and treating the unbeliever as if he or she wasn't so valuable? After all, the thinking goes, the Bible doesn't describe unbelievers as being as precious to the Lord as believers. Perhaps non-Christians don't deserve gracious communication. But what is the spiritual state of people who aren't Christians? They are spiritually dead sinners in need of the same grace in Christ that believers have found. Yes, they deserve God's punishment. But no, Christians should never give them a foretaste of that condemnation through their harsh, judgmental attitudes. Apart from the grace of God in Christ, Christians deserve the same hell as non-Christians. Gracious, loving words should flow from the mouths of those who have received grace from the Lord. Maybe the extension of the Lord's grace through a Christian in his or her communication to a non-Christian will become the means that the Lord will use to bring His saving grace to the unbeliever as well.

In a context of Christian suffering, Peter called on his readers to stand strong and honor Jesus Christ while being treated unjustly. He explained that sometimes the godly reactions of believers in the midst of trials will arrest the attention of non-Christians, provoking them to inquire about the reason for the Christians' hope. At these times Christians ought to speak up for Christ, but do so with grace. As the apostle put it in 1 Peter 3:14–16: "But even if you should suffer for righteousness' sake, you are blessed. 'And do not be afraid of their threats, nor be troubled.' But sanctify the Lord God in your hearts, and always be ready to give a defense to everyone who asks you a reason for the hope that is in you, with meekness and fear; having a good conscience, that when they defame you as evildoers, those who revile your good conduct in Christ may be ashamed."

Check Your Posture

What posture should Christians assume when they relate to other people? Your posture is your attitude or disposition toward those around you. Is the other person a friend or an enemy—is he or she a teammate or a competitor? A person with an adversarial attitude participating in a conversation increases the potential for hostility. Consider the impact of your assumptions about others when engaging them in discussions.

Suppose two fierce competitors send salesmen to get a company to buy their products. The company representative, however, has time only to meet with both salesmen at the same time. Would you expect the salesmen to extend love and graciousness toward each other during the meeting? Will the rivals go the extra mile to assume the best about the motives behind each other's statements? Will all of the hearts involved be on guard against vices that could come out in sarcasm or severe tones?

How would the conversation change if the three participants were great friends who co-owned a company and were comparing research on the products they needed? In both of these scenarios different products with various strengths and weaknesses are discussed. Each of the people makes valid points based on their perspectives—often bringing passion to the table. But which of the two conversations is most likely to be marked by kindness and consideration? Obviously, when everyone is on the same team, or perceives themselves to be on the same team, the potential for a gracious and effective conversation multiplies exponentially. Consider the contrast between newlyweds sweetly working through their bare-bones budget and then years later that same couple on the brink of divorce wrestling over the division of assets. All of the sweetness dissolves when their posture changes from love and friendship to bitter enemies.

If two people are having a theological discussion, it makes a difference if they posture themselves as enemies or friends. Are they on the same team working it out together? Or are they sitting on opposite sides of the table, mixing in verbal jabs and insults alongside their biblical insights? Why not strive, if at all possible, to stay on the same side of the table, working together to solve the issue? If two people recognize that they have a common goal, it will help them to use warm and gentle tones as they communicate with each other.

Sometimes Christians are forced into adversarial situations. Moreover, Jesus acknowledges the potential for enemies when He says in the Sermon on the Mount that we should love our enemies and pray for our persecutors (Matt. 5:44). But Paul reminds us, "If it is possible, as much as depends on you, live peaceably with all men" (Rom. 12:18). While there is often more people can do to promote peace in a conflict, these verses leave room for life in a fallen world—sometimes it will not be possible to be at peace with a person. In any situation, however, you will find it easier to cultivate gracious speech if you endeavor to avoid an adversarial posture as much as possible. When it comes to fellow church members and fellow brothers and sisters in the body of Christ, we should not be opposed to each other. All believers should approach theological and personal issues together with the gracious posture of those on the Lord's team.

Christian mediator Ken Sande applies this principle to the context of dealing with another person's sins. He says:

> When you need to show others their faults, do not talk down to them as though you are faultless and they are inferior to you. Instead, talk with them as though you are standing side by side at the foot of the cross. Acknowledge your present, ongoing need for the Savior. Admit ways that you have wrestled with the same or other sins or weaknesses, and give hope by describing how God has forgiven you and is currently working in you to help you change.... When people sense this kind of humility and common bond, they will be less inclined to react to correction with pride and defensiveness.[1]

Remember the Golden Rule

Contrary to the well-worn pun, the Golden Rule is not "he who has the gold makes the rules." The Golden Rule, which is to treat others as you would like to be treated, actually comes from our Lord Jesus in His Sermon on the Mount. Matthew 7:12 says, "Therefore, whatever you want men to do to you, do also to them, for this is the Law and the Prophets." Ponder the Golden Rule's application to the discussion about gracious speech. When you seek to cultivate kindness, you must think about the ways you like to be treated. How do you want others to speak to you? Do you like it when people speak in harsh and condemning tones, even when they are saying true things? Do you think it is personally helpful when somebody has a bit of important truth for you to hear, but they communicate

---

1. Sande, *Peacemaker: A Biblical Guide*, 172.

it like a carpenter attacks wood with his nail gun? Not many hearers appreciate that kind of delivery. Jesus says to His followers, "If you don't like this kind of approach, you should not use it with others." Remembering the Golden Rule is an effective means of cultivating graciousness.

Reformed theologian Roger Nicole wrote an article titled "How to Deal with Those Who Differ from Us" about engaging in discussions with people who have different theological perspectives. Using Jesus's Golden Rule, Nicole asserted that before trying to win arguments, believers must consider their obligations to those with whom they differ:

> This does not involve agreeing with them. We have an obligation to the truth that has priority over agreement with any particular person; if someone is not in the truth, we have no right to agree. We have no right even to minimize the importance of the difference; and therefore, we do not owe consent, and we do not owe indifference. But what we owe that person who differs from us, whoever that may be, is what we owe every human being—*we owe them to love them.* And we owe them to deal with them as we ourselves would like to be dealt with or treated (Matthew 7:12).[2]

Become a Better Listener

The Lord gave clear instructions about the connection between the heart and the mouth, but there is also a connection between the ear and the mouth. Being a better listener

---

2. Roger Nicole, "How to Deal with Those Who Differ from Us," in Bailey, *Speaking the Truth in Love*, 184.

helps you become more gracious in several ways. First, listening well shows respect for the person in the conversation. The brother for whom Christ died or the sinner in need of the grace Christians have received deserves a respectful ear. Listening itself shows respect, but it also puts the listener in a mind-set of respect. Good listening also expresses that you value the ideas of the one who is talking. As we have seen, placing a high value on the speaker and what she is saying directly impacts the level of your care in choosing gracious responses. In dealing with a person in a ministry context who talks incessantly, David Powlison counsels counselors: "The first part of the process looks easy. You have little choice in the matter. You listen. Here's the hard part: you do have a choice about *how* you listen. Listen well. Don't go numb; don't just go along; don't get irritated; don't run for the exit. Listen so you'll understand. Understand so you'll be able to talk with well-aimed words of life, so you'll know how to love."[3]

Second, listening helps us understand people better. Knowing the backgrounds, concerns, and questions behind a question or comment helps you temper your tone. For example, if you are conversing with someone who believes that people can lose their salvation, you should first listen between the lines, discern his real concerns, and listen to what he means more than just what he says before attempting to present biblical evidence to prove that true believers cannot lose their salvation. In other words, it helps to discover the reasons he or she is so passionate about this issue. If you merely match passion and volume for passion and volume,

---

3. David Powlison, *Speaking Truth in Love: Counsel in Community* (Winston-Salem, N.C.: Punch Press, 2005), 85.

coupled with verses against verses, what do you think will be accomplished? Will God be glorified? Will the conversation communicate the love of Christ to the other person?

If, on the other hand, you truly listen before you speak, you may sense, for example, a deep concern that a person who believes in eternal security would lack motivation to live for God. The speaker's distress is not as much with your set of verses as it is a positive concern for personal holiness. As long as the speaker assumes that you believe that Christians can do whatever they want—"once saved, always saved"—the conversation will probably not be fruitful, no matter how strong the arguments. So many times in theological debates, a Christian can become overbearing instead of being a careful listener. A good listener can become a more gracious speaker by addressing the concerns behind the questions, which will often diffuse tension and lead to a better conversation about the original question. After you affirm the Bible's mandate for personal holiness and that holiness is a fruit of true salvation, the other person will probably be much more open to discussing verses about eternal security.

Third, listening provides time to pause and consider the conversation. Another way to cultivate graciousness is to stop and think before speaking. Listening well helps the hearer slow down to consider questions like, What is this person really saying? How should I best respond to his point? What would God have me to say? Is this the best time to respond? How would God want me to say it? Nicole cautions, "Rather than preparing ourselves to pounce on that person the moment he or she stops talking, we should concentrate on apprehending precisely what the other person holds."[4]

A fourth way listening allows you to be more gracious is by helping you to express the other person's point of view. It is a good goal to understand the other person so well that you can give his perspective in such a way that he will be pleased with the presentation. Many hearers disregard what you say if they don't think you have correctly understood them. Nicole describes having this goal in the midst of a theological disagreement: "Then my aim was to represent the view faithfully and fully without mingling the criticism with factual statements; in fact, so faithfully and fully that an adherent to that position might comment, 'This man certainly does understand our view!' It would be a special boon if one could say, 'I never heard it stated better!' This then could earn me the right to criticize."[5]

Most people appreciate it when the other person in a conflict or debate carefully listens, can accurately express the speaker's perspective, and then interacts with it. Communications professor Tim Muehlhoff conveys urgency over this point as he cautions, "We need to avoid pretending to understand a person's perspective if we really don't."[6] He calls such an approach "pseudo-listening." Muehlhoff offers the experienced advice of asking clarifying questions with a gracious tone and attitude, and then offering a summary statement of

---

4. Nicole, "How to Deal with Those Who Differ from Us," in Bailey, *Speaking the Truth in Love*, 185.

5. Nicole, "How to Deal with Those Who Differ from Us," in Bailey, *Speaking the Truth in Love*, 188.

6. Tim Muehlhoff, *I Beg to Differ: Navigating Difficult Conversations with Truth and Love* (Downers Grove, Ill.: IVP, 2014), 95.

the other person's narrative, giving him the opportunity to further clarify his position if needed.[7]

Finally, listening well helps you achieve effective communication, and it shows love to the other person. Nicole encourages participants in biblical debates to demonstrate that they have a real interest in one another—an eagerness to learn from each other as well as to help each other.[8] The Bible says, "A fool has no delight in understanding, but in expressing his own heart" (Prov. 18:2). In other words, fools never listen well, because they don't love others. Instead, fools spout their own ideas and assumptions, because they are obsessed with themselves.

Make Charitable Judgments

If you love someone, you discipline your mind to assume the best about that person's words or actions until you have the facts to prove otherwise.[9] While such mental discipline may not seem to fit modern sentimental concepts of love, according to the Bible, love means sacrificing one's own wants to meet the needs of another (John 15:12–14). The real opposite of love is not hate, but selfishness. Instead of selfishly assuming that you know everything about the thoughts and motivations behind the other person's words or actions, in love you should selflessly assume the best interpretation of what the other person has said or done. This idea flows from Paul's description of love in 1 Corinthians 13:7: love "bears all things, believes

---

7. Muehlhoff, *I Beg to Differ*, 95–96.

8. Nicole, "How to Deal with Those Who Differ from Us," in Bailey, *Speaking the Truth in Love*, 188.

9. Sande, *Peacemaker: A Biblical Guide*, 171.

all things, hopes all things, endures all things." Because you are called by God to love your fellow Christians, family members, neighbors, and even your enemies, you should assume the best of everyone.

In times of conflict, the participants' presuppositions will become evident, for good or bad, leading to better or worse outcomes. When one person in the conversation looks at the other through sunglasses, everything will be tinted darker. Ken Sande observes, "If people sense that you have jumped to conclusions about them and enjoy finding fault in them, they are likely to resist correction. If, on the other hand, they sense that you are trying to believe the best about them, they will be more inclined to listen to your concerns."[10]

Think about the Practical Outcomes
Think about the ways that different styles of speaking during a conversation can make things worse or better. If a group of typical coworkers discusses where to have lunch, everyone might quickly settle on a pizza place. But if that group includes self-appointed pizza aficionados, more dialogue may be required to ensure you are eating the right kind of pizza for the mood and moment. While members of the group may offer a variety of positive considerations, moving toward a good decision, what will happen if one of the passionate pizza experts becomes emotional and unkind? It could add fuel to the fire. If a second coworker insults the first "expert's" favorite place, they could become vexed with one another. Suddenly, pizza is not the issue anymore as the expert is thinking about the ways that his pizza was disparaged. He fires back about

---

10. Sande, *Peacemaker: A Biblical Guide*, 170.

the critical coworker's lack of taste. Instead of getting closer to satisfying everyone's appetite, the second coworker begins thinking of zingers to put the first one in his place. Soon the other coworkers slip away and eat Chinese food.

When discussing any issue, from pizza to parenting or from movies to money, graciousness helps you and the other participants concentrate on the issues at hand instead of clouding them over with emotional reactions. In addition to avoiding the hindrances that harshness can cause, gracious answers smoothly direct the conversation toward solutions. Once again the book of Proverbs offers wise insights on the matter:

> A soft answer turns away wrath, but a harsh word stirs up anger. (15:1)

> A wholesome tongue is a tree of life, but perverseness in it breaks the spirit. (15:4)

> A wrathful man stirs up strife, but he who is slow to anger allays contention. (15:18)

> The wise in heart will be called prudent, and sweetness of the lips increases learning. (16:21)

The letter of James has been called the Proverbs of the New Testament. James also acknowledges the power of the tongue to produce powerful outcomes:

> Even so the tongue is a little member and boasts great things.
>
> See how great a forest a little fire kindles! And the tongue is a fire, a world of iniquity. The tongue is so set among our members that it defiles the whole body, and sets on fire the course of nature; and it is

set on fire by hell. For every kind of beast and bird, of reptile and creature of the sea, is tamed and has been tamed by mankind. But no man can tame the tongue. It is an unruly evil, full of deadly poison. With it we bless our God and Father, and with it we curse men, who have been made in the similitude of God. Out of the same mouth proceed blessing and cursing. My brethren, these things ought not to be so. (3:5–10)

Outcomes are better when graciousness seasons the means. In order to experience the best possible results of conversations, you should use sweetness of speech. Intentionally considering the outcome you desire from an interaction will help you cultivate the best means of getting to the goal. If you are ungracious, mean, and harsh, the talk will generally end badly. To quote Sande, "Strong words are more likely to evoke defensiveness and antagonism, and once a conversation takes on this tone, it is difficult to move to a friendlier plane."[11] Your tone of voice can turn a routine conversation into a fight. But if you use soft, sweet, and kind tones, expressions, and words, a conversation will bless everyone involved.

Conclusion

While a bull has no hope of successfully navigating through the narrow aisles of a china shop—no matter how much training it receives—Christians can make real progress in becoming gracious. Just as farmers work for a harvest, first below the soil, preparing the land and sowing the seeds, and then above the soil, helping the plants to become fruitful, so Christians can work for a harvest of graciousness, first below

---

11. Sande, *Peacemaker: A Biblical Guide*, 171.

the surface in their hearts, changing their thoughts and attitudes, and then out of their hearts, changing their behaviors. The Lord Jesus does not simply forgive His unkind children; through the Holy Spirit He also changes them into kind children. By using the personal strategies for cultivating graciousness considered in this chapter, the believer can anticipate genuine change.

Chapter 8

Cultivating Graciousness through Your Actions

Most of the kindness-producing practices identified so far could be compared to a farmer preparing land and sowing seeds—heart shifts replace wrong patterns of thinking and reacting with thought patterns that inspire a harvest of graciousness. After the faithful farmer has scattered seeds, he will use means to help the sprouts grow strong and fruitful, such as applying fertilizers, removing weeds and bugs, and even using stakes to support tender shoots. In addition to the various heart shifts we have considered that are necessary for cultivating and seeding the soil of our hearts, there are practical means of supporting and strengthening gracious practices for those who desire to become kind and gentle. The farmer happily uses practical helps to get the most out of the harvest. In this chapter, we will consider practical means for achieving a fruitful harvest of graciousness.

Think Before Speaking

My wife once made this simple but profound observation: "If I would just think about what I want to say before I say it, I would sin less." Certainly, this maxim applies to the way we deliver our words as much as their content. You should not issue your words in a thoughtless manner; you should stop and think before speaking. You should briefly ask questions like, who am I addressing? In his consideration of Ephesians 4:29, which says that all our speech should be helpful for building others up, Paul Tripp recommends a series of questions to consider about the person we are addressing, each of which could affect the way we proceed with a conversation:

> To whom are we speaking? Is it a man, woman, boy, or girl? Is it someone our own age, younger, or older? Is it a long-time friend, a casual acquaintance, or a virtual stranger? Is it a family member, a distant relative, or a neighbor? Is the person a believer, a seeker, or lost? What is his or her knowledge and experience of the truths of Scripture? How receptive is this person to my ministry? How do the answers to these questions guide me in what to say?[1]

Another important question to consider is, *what needs to be said?* Take the time to consider the person, her situation, and the content that needs to be communicated. The more you learn about the person you are addressing, including her background and life situation, the better chance you have at offering targeted, helpful, upbuilding words. Paul recognized that different people in different situations require different communication. He told the Thessalonians, "Now we exhort you, brethren, warn those who are unruly, comfort the fainthearted, uphold the weak, be patient with all" (1 Thess. 5:14). Paul advises three different medicines for people in three different conditions, with patience applied to everyone. The

---

1. Tripp, *War of Words*, 237.

more we think about the person we are addressing, the more we realize how complex that person is—she is filled with different attitudes and assumptions. As we develop a more complex understanding of the person we are addressing, we also develop empathy for her, which adds to the graciousness in our communication.[2]

Closely related to the person's background and the contents of our conversation is the timing of the discussion. Think about this question: *Are there any factors that affect the timing of the conversation?* As Sande says, "Timing is an essential ingredient of effective communication. If possible, do not discuss sensitive matters with someone who is tired, worried about other things, or in a bad mood. Nor should you approach someone about an important concern unless you will have enough time to discuss the matter thoroughly."[3]

In addition to concerns about timing, Sande advises thoughtfulness about the place of the conversation. He cautions about having a conversation while others are present; avoiding loud, distracting noises; and ensuring that the person you are addressing feels secure.[4] Any of these factors can dramatically impact a discussion, yet with minimal forethought, we can anticipate background, timing, and setting and accommodate the person we are talking to.

Am I thinking about God? In the midst of navigating difficult discussions, keeping God in the forefront of our thoughts is the wisest thing we can do. When we consider God, it follows that we will also be contemplating His word. These

---

2. Muehlhoff, *I Beg to Differ*, 114.
3. Sande, *Peacemaker: A Biblical Guide*, 173.
4. Sande, *Peacemaker: A Biblical Guide*, 173.

kinds of Godward thoughts inspire graciousness by reminding us of God's graciousness, His commands to be loving and gentle, and His promises to help us to become gracious.

Additionally, several verses from Proverbs remind us of the wisdom of knowing whether it is even wise for us to speak out:

> In the multitude of words sin is not lacking, but he who restrains his lips is wise. (10:19)

> He who has knowledge spares his words, and a man of understanding is of a calm spirit. (17:27)

> Do you see a man hasty in his words? There is more hope for a fool than for him. (29:20)

A wise heart waits before allowing words to leave the mouth.

Because of the pipeline that exists between a fallen heart and mouth, words that flow from you are guaranteed, at times, to be sinful. My wise wife was exactly right, though. Stopping to think provides you a much better chance of responding in a gracious, sweet, and wise way than when you merely react emotionally and begin to speak with harsh tones shaped by a critical attitude.

Use a Journal

Writing in a journal can be a wonderful means for Christians to cultivate spiritual growth in their lives. It can help you slow down to express the ways the Lord is working in your life, and reviewing the entries you've made over time can reveal larger patterns of thinking and behavior.[5] Additionally, you can use

---

5. See Donald S. Whitney, *Spiritual Disciplines for the Christian Life*, rev. ed. (Colorado Springs: NavPress, 2014), 249–70.

a journal in a more focused way to work on specific struggles such as worry, depression, or, what we are considering here, unkindness.

When you experience an episode of harshness, it is helpful to write down the details of it as soon as possible, while it is fresh in your thoughts. You should write down a few lines about the circumstances of the outburst, but most importantly, you should write down what you were thinking and wanting as the events unfolded. Later, when your emotional reactions have calmed, you should review your records, possibly including a wise friend in the process. The goal is to compare the thoughts of your heart with the ways the Scriptures enjoin believers to think and act in such situations. With quieted emotions, it is easier to become objective in the analysis.

For example, if Lisa and Jennifer argue in the parking lot after a church meeting about involving a new visitor in the ladies' ministry, they might be so filled with emotions like anger, embarrassment, and even shame that they have difficulty remembering what led to the conflict. At lunch, however, Jennifer takes a few minutes to write down some of her thoughts in bullet points. Later that afternoon, perhaps after a nap, she pulls out her notes. She can then see more clearly that she has not been thinking according to the Scriptures. Now she realizes that her thoughts were prideful: "Lisa doesn't like me or the people I want to recruit for the ladies' ministry"; "I want my new friend included right away"; and "I'm going to really let Lisa have it." Now that the emotional dust has settled, she can contrast her earlier thoughts with thoughts that correspond to biblical graciousness.

In Ephesians 4, Paul appeals to the church at Ephesus to be united on the basis of the gospel truths he had taught them in chapters 1–3. He commends gracious virtues as a vital means of maintaining Christian unity. Paul charges the church to "walk worthy of the calling with which you were called, with all lowliness and gentleness, with longsuffering, bearing with one another in love, endeavoring to keep the unity of the Spirit in the bond of peace" (4:1–3). The unity charge to the church along with the means to maintain that unity has clear applications for people struggling with fellow church members. As Jennifer compares her thoughts to the inspired words of Paul, she repents and literally writes out new, humble thoughts to guide her thinking the next time she interacts with Lisa. She writes out thoughts like, "I must love Lisa far more than I want to get my way in this ministry"; and "Even though I am eager to see my friend become more involved, I should be patient with the process and the people making the decisions"; and "However this works out, I need to honor the Lord and pursue unity with my sisters in Christ." Humble biblical thoughts produce gracious communication with others. Using a journal in this way can help you identify and replace unkind ways of thinking and acting with thoughts and deeds that please the Lord.

Use Gracious Helper Words

In order to create habits of gracious speaking, you should incorporate words and phrases into your dialogue designed to remind you of the need to be more gracious and to be a conduit of kindness. Expressions such as "I think," "it seems," or "from my perspective" acknowledge that you are aware you lack omniscience. While everyone else knows that you don't know everything, it is good for the people you address to hear you affirm that you don't know everything. A major reason people are harsh, critical, and severe is that they sincerely believe they are right. Because harsh speakers are so confident in their opinions, they feel no need or desire to say, "It *seems* this way"; instead, they say, "It *is* this way!"

Regardless of how often you are right, no one is always right. While you may be certain about many biblical truths, when you discuss them you should use humble phrases to genuinely help you to remain humble and further the conversation. Since no human being has all of the information in the universe, it is generally a helpful habit to express opinions by showing some deference to the listener or reader—for example, "It *seems* like this is the way it is"; "It *seems* like this is what this verse is saying"; "I *think* that this verse connects with that verse in this way to give us this doctrine"; "*From my perspective*, that seems to be the direction to go."

Humility can acknowledge your limitations and then soften your expressions with your tones and manner, allowing your message to be better received. So, for example, if you get into a dialogue about a challenging teaching from the Bible, like God's sovereignty in salvation, you could say true things in different ways, which often leads to different results with the hearer. You could directly present some of the plainest statements in Romans 9 and Ephesians 1 and then make dogmatic declarations about God choosing some for salvation from eternity past and passing over others. In this style of conversation, you are not overly concerned about your hearers, their backgrounds, their concerns, or their questions—you just take aim with your Bible gun and fire away. After all, God is sovereign, so He will handle the results anyway. Muehlhoff describes this dynamic as being position centered as opposed to being person centered.[6] If, on the other hand, you first acknowledge your lack of omniscience by expressing the same thoughts and opinions in a softer way, the conversation may be more beneficial to both parties. If you say, "*As I read* this verse in Romans 9, *I think* it is teaching that there is a distinction between God's attitude and actions from eternity past toward Jacob and Esau. His eternal plan for dealing with these two individuals *seems to* come from His sovereign plan rather than from what either of them would do or believe later in their lives."

Notice that with this style of communicating with more humble words and tones, there is no alteration or softening of the truth. There seems to be a connection between the use of softer words and tones and moving the conversation forward in a positive, interactive way. But when you are critical, harsh, and offensive in your wording or unnecessarily dogmatic, your hearers often close the door and shut out further input from you, and your relationship suffers. If a conversation style causes relationships to suffer, are those involved being loving and Christlike? If you are not being loving and Christlike, Jesus Christ has something to say about you and the way you represent His truth. Softer words are a humble acknowledgment that you do not know every fact in the universe. Gracious helper words provide a good reminder to you, and they help your listeners hear the intended message, thereby guiding the conversation to progress in a more beneficial direction.

---

6. Muehlhoff, *I Beg to Differ*, 147.

Remember That Everything Communicates

Even when your mouth is not moving, you are communicating. A husband who grunts over his glowing iPad as his wife tries to sort through a discipline issue with one of the children is accused of not being a good communicator. In fact, this husband is an excellent communicator. Although a few words of acknowledgment do make it across his lips, everything else about his expression, mannerism, and eye gaze communicates disinterest; he sends the message of disengagement effectively, and his wife receives it loudly and clearly. In order to cultivate graciousness, you need to be conscious of the significance of nonverbal communication and make use of it to enhance the communication of kindness.

In a letter to a mother of several children who was trying to promote pleasantness in her busy home, Sam Crabtree offers a list of the benefits of a positive tone of voice: "It wins friends. It builds confidence in the minds of others that they can trust you. It demonstrates maturity (read James 3:3–12). It sweetens the ambiance, the atmosphere, the environment; it makes you easier to be around."[7]

Longtime pastor's wife Mary Beeke adds more detail to the simple yet significant effects of nonverbal communication:

> Tone of voice and facial expression are huge factors. They express patience, tolerance, kindness, and happiness—or a lack thereof. When Mom says, "Come here, Brian," her tone can convey either irritation or cheerfulness. When I am around a person with indomitable cheerfulness, I am uplifted; I feel

---

7. Sam Crabtree, *Practicing Affirmation: God-Centered Praise of Those Who Are Not God* (Wheaton, Ill.: Crossway, 2011), 166.

safe, accepted, and comfortable in his or her presence. Wouldn't it be great if we all had that effect on each other? If we wish to improve our communication skills, this is the area to begin with that will make the most impact. By simply being aware of how we sound and our impact on others, we can take steps to change. It might involve dealing with underlying issues, but that is another subject. If we shore up the self-discipline it takes to be cheerful, our emotions may just follow along.[8]

If your nonverbal communication contradicts your verbal communication, which one cancels out the other? If a husband tells his wife she is beautiful and sweetly gives her a bouquet of flowers with a warm smile as he tells her of his undying love, the effect of his message multiplies. If he mopes in the door, rolls his eyes, and yawns as he mumbles about his undying love while he picks up the newspaper before finishing his sentence, all the refreshing romance of his words will evaporate. Corresponding nonverbal communication strengthens your words, but contradictory nonverbal communication neutralizes, and even nullifies, your words. In order to cultivate graciousness, you must be aware of the power of nonverbal communication. There are humorous stories about people saying embarrassing things without realizing that a microphone was still on. In a similar way, everyone broadcasts continuous messages through their tones, facial expressions, and other nonverbal gestures, whether they realize their "mic" is live or not. Those seeking to become tenderhearted should

---

8. Mary Beeke, *The Law of Kindness: Serving with Heart and Hands* (Grand Rapids: Reformation Heritage Books, 2007), 180–81.

intentionally use gentle manners and tones to multiply the impact of gracious words.

Beg God for Grace to Be Gracious

God wills for His children to become gracious, and you have a wonderful resource at your disposal to grow in graciousness—prayer. Whenever you pray according to God's will, God promises to answer those requests positively: "Now this is the confidence that we have in Him, that if we ask anything according to His will, He hears us. And if we know that He hears us, whatever we ask, we know that we have the petitions that we have asked of Him" (1 John 5:14–15). Asking God to make you more gracious is a prayer according to God's will. Therefore, God guarantees that He will answer such a prayer to make you more gracious.

For a time, I worked with a fellow Christian who had an organizational style different from mine. The time in my life that we interacted was extremely busy for me. As I assisted him, he regularly did things that, in my view, did not seem like the best use of our time. The temptation to be impatient and frustrated loomed large over my heart. Frustration, irritation, and impatience in hearts are like the electricity building within dark storm clouds—lightning will soon strike. I recognized this dangerous charge within my own heart. In order to escape the potential lightning bolts I was anticipating, I began praying for my relationship with this man. Every day during that time I prayed that God would knit my heart together in love with the heart of this fellow believer (in Colossians 2:2 Paul prays for believers "that their hearts may be encouraged, being knit together in love"). What prayer request could be more in line with God's will than to love another Christian from my heart?

After about a month, I forgot about those prayers. I didn't think about my urgent request to God until the day this person unleashed another, in my mind, organizational mess-up. What reminded me about my prayer request was my response to the situation. I didn't mind the man's new plan at all. I experienced no impatience or irritation. There was no choking back harsh, thunderous tones in my reply. What made the difference? I was filled with a divinely born love for the man; I loved him so much that I didn't care about the way he wanted to plan compared to how I would have planned. We became much better friends after that. God never supernaturally changed this man's organizational style, but He supernaturally changed my heart. God answered my prayers, which were according to His will.

As a spider's web connects and strengthens itself at many different points, there are many connections between gracious speech and the fruit of the Holy Spirit: "But the fruit of the Spirit is love, joy, peace, longsuffering, kindness, goodness, faithfulness, gentleness, self-control. Against such there is no law" (Gal. 5:22–23). Paul itemized these virtues to help the Galatian churches identify true believers and false teachers. The fruit of the Spirit is a cluster of ripe fruit that the Holy Spirit works into the hearts and lives of believers. Every part of the Holy Spirit's fruit will have a sweetening effect on your speech. New love for a fellow Christian made it much easier for me to speak to him kindly, even as we discussed organizational differences. How can you be mean if you are filled with God's joy? Patience is always an antidote to an angry edge in a conversation. Kindness, goodness, and gentleness are parallel terms for being gracious. The Holy Spirit will help you faithfully follow our Lord's example in using self-control with your tongue. If the Holy Spirit already specializes in working these kinds of virtues into the hearts of believers in general ways, there is great reason to hope that God is ready, willing, and able to quickly answer your prayers for a more gracious mouth.

King David prayed in Psalm 19:14:

> Let the words of my mouth and the meditation of
> my heart
> Be acceptable in Your sight,
> O LORD, my strength and my Redeemer.

In Psalm 141:3, he prayed, "Set a guard, O LORD, over my mouth; keep watch over the door of my lips." You can see from David's example that these kinds of prayers are not a novel practice; God's people have been saying them for a long time. God has heard these requests before. He has answered them before, and He will answer them again. Perhaps like me, you will pray about your tones and words for a while and then forget that you have done it. Hopefully, later you will remember your prayer as someone remarks about how much more gracious you have become. Christians who experience answers to their prayers should remember to thank God for working change in their hearts.

Use the Bible Thoroughly

The chief means the Holy Spirit uses to transform God's children into greater conformity to the image of Jesus Christ is the Scriptures. The inspired Scriptures guide Christians in renewing their minds in order to live in all the ways that please the Lord (Rom. 12:1–2). While most Christians are aware of the importance of reading the Bible regularly, they often fall short of appreciating and using the full array of resources God's Word provides. To make significant progress in heart-level transformation toward graciousness, you must maximize your Bible intake. In addition to consistently reading the Bible, there are several other helpful disciplines that will exponentially elevate the transforming benefits of the Bible in your life.[9]

Meditate on the Scriptures

Overcoming the sin remaining in your heart that frequently finds ways to slip out between your lips requires more than mere human help. Bad attitudes in our hearts are the result of patterns of sinful thoughts clustered together. In order to change the sinful thoughts emerging as bad attitudes that season our speech, we need to conform our thinking to the transforming Scriptures. As Joshua was preparing to lead God's people into war against God's enemies, the chief weapon for success God gave Joshua was a mind filled with the Bible: "This Book of the Law shall not depart from your mouth, but you shall meditate in it day and night, that you may observe to do according to all that is written in it. For then you will make your way prosperous, and then you will have good success" (Josh. 1:8). The godly man of Psalm 1 enjoyed the blessings of perpetual fruitfulness because of his prior commitment to meditate perpetually on the word of God:

> Blessed is the man
> Who walks not in the counsel of the ungodly,
>> Nor stands in the path of sinners,
>> Nor sits in the seat of the scornful;

---

9. See Whitney, *Spiritual Disciplines for the Christian Life*, 21–78.

But his delight is in the law of the LORD,
And in His law he meditates day and night. (vv. 1–2)

Taking time to ponder the meaning and applications of any portion of the Bible is fruitful for spiritual progress, but identifying sections of the Bible that specifically relate to godly communication will aggressively target your heart in the areas of gentleness, kindness, and sweetness. You should list the key verses that directly address the particular heart issues and temptations you are fighting against. One person is tempted to be harsh, critical, or too sharp in different ways from others. What are the personal "buttons" that ignite your harsh speech? Think deeply about the specific Scripture passages that are most helpful in addressing and changing those specific heart issues.

For example, if someone believed that sinfully passionate assertions are the best way to change other people's behavior, an excellent biblical remedy would be Paul's instruction to Timothy in 2 Timothy 2:24–26 about correcting in gentleness and patience, because it is God who grants repentance. To experience more profound levels of transformation, the believer must not be content with a surface reading of the verses. Just as a colorful piece of hard candy changes the color of the tongue as it slowly dissolves, so these verses will color the heart of the one who spends time thinking about, appreciating, and applying them. Writing down meditation insights adds even more impact and allows you in the future to build on the treasures you discover.[10]

---

10. For more ideas about meditating on Scripture, see David W. Saxton, *God's Battle Plan for the Mind: The Puritan Practice of Biblical Meditation* (Grand Rapids: Reformation Heritage Books, 2015).

Pray through Scripture

This spiritual discipline can go hand in hand with meditation. As God reveals Himself and His ways to His child through meditation on His word, the Christian can respond in prayer. There are many profitable directions you could take as you respond to a portion of Scripture in prayer. For example, meditating on 2 Timothy 2:24–26 could prompt several avenues for prayer. You could be convicted about your lack of gentleness or patience in correcting another person, leading you to confess your sins to the Lord. You might also make intercession to the God who grants repentance for specific individuals in need of correction. Your petitions might be based on a renewed desire to handle cases requiring correction graciously. Your recognition of God's sovereign power in changing others could lead you to praise and thanksgiving. Prayers affirming your trust in God could rise as you are reminded of the spiritual war that takes place as the devil holds sinners captive. Using Christ's word as a basis for communing with Him is an excellent means of driving the truth deeper into your heart. The Holy Spirit loves to use the tool of truth and the prayers of God's people as means of spiritual growth and change.[11]

Listen to Sermons about Graciousness

The best sermons identify the point of a passage or passages of Scripture and teach and apply those truths to the hearers. In every age the Lord has raised up gifted men to proclaim His Word to congregations of Christians. Unlike past generations, however, many Christians living in the twenty-first

---

11. See Donald S. Whitney, *Praying the Bible* (Wheaton, Ill: Crossway, 2015).

century have unprecedented access through the Internet to expository sermons from all over the world. Many websites, smartphone applications, and search engines can direct hearers to messages on specific passages of or topics from the Bible. After you have meditated on a passage, imagine the fruitfulness of hearing the insights of gifted preachers on the same text. The inspired Scriptures can be rightly considered and applied in many ways, so listening to sermons can add depth and breadth to your understanding of the Bible's teachings on graciousness, as well as provide more ways to apply the lessons you have learned.

Memorize Key Passages of the Bible
Memorizing the Bible provides a tool for continual meditation because you can reflect on a passage any time and in any place. In addition to Scripture passages that directly relate to graciousness, other general biblical promises can be a vital help in spiritual transformation. Because of remaining sin, even those believers who fully intend to cultivate lovingkindness in their relationships will experience setbacks. There will be occasions when other people will pull the trigger that results in harsh reaction, and the sincerest believer will respond sinfully. At such times, in addition to being thoroughly aware of the Bible's teachings about graciousness, you will also have immediate access to the spiritual encouragement of some of God's promises.

For example, if you memorized 1 John 1:9 you could be assured that if you confess your bad attitudes and harsh communication to God, He will cleanse you from all unrighteousness. Knowing 1 Corinthians 10:13 by heart assures you that you will never be overwhelmed by any temptation and that God will supply all the grace you need for endurance. The promise of God's abiding presence in Hebrews 13:5 comforts believers in all kinds of situations. Many times the urge to react with an angry retort can be averted if we remember that God is present in the situation. Romans 8:28–30 has comforted Christians from the first century on that God is always working out His plan in the lives of those who love Him and are called according to His purpose. God's plan is for His glory and the ultimate good of His people. Having promises like these at the ready through advanced memorization will help encourage you in the battle to be like Jesus Christ, who is full of grace and truth.

Chapter 9

Cultivating Graciousness in Community

Christianity is more like a team sport, such as basketball, football, or soccer, than an individual sport, such as golf, bowling, or tennis. Certainly team sports require efforts from individual members of the team; the more outstanding the individuals perform, the better the results the team will achieve. Individual sports can also have team components, with coaches and others striving to help the participants do their best, but success or failure in individual sports rests on the single player.

Some individual Christians wrongly act as if the results of their Christian character and ministry rest completely on them. While the Holy Spirit is God's agent of spiritual growth and Christians are called to take responsibility to work out the implications of their salvation (Phil. 2:12–13), individual Christians are not called by God to do these things in isolation. Christians are called to live, grow, and serve within a believing community—a church. As with a body, each part makes contributions to the health and effectiveness of the whole (Rom. 12:4–8; 1 Cor. 12:14–27). Like the individuals on a team, each member in the church has a specialized role to play to help the team win the game. Not everyone on a basketball team is small, fast, and can shoot a basket a long distance away from the goal. Not everyone is tall and strong, able to get rebounds and make shots through defenders right under the rim. But when each player uses his or her abilities, it compensates for the others' deficiencies. An outstanding team of men or women, each performing their roles well and precisely working together for the common goal, performs like one great person.

The Bible speaks of the ministry of church members to one another for the spiritual benefits of the whole body of Christ (Eph. 4:11–16). The gifts and spiritual experiences of various church members show forth differently. One believer within a church can strengthen the weakness of another Christian. The Christian limited in one area makes wonderful contributions to the rest of the body in another area. The church team works together to accomplish far more than any individual could accomplish alone. For example, Samuel may not be an effective teacher, but he has excellent knowledge of and skills for setting up the meeting place for church gatherings, and this is how he serves others. Steven may not have much time to offer, but he earns a large amount of money in his job and has tremendous faith, which shows itself in the way he gives generously to the work of the church. George has fought hard to overcome battles with pornography and has the desire and ability to help other men with similar struggles. Holly makes difficult biblical truths simple for children, helping parents equip their children with God's word. Depression had Dave down for many months, but now that he is through the trial, he reaches out to his discouraged friends Boyd and Nicholas with the hope he found in the Scriptures. Experiences in life and with the

Lord, knowledge of the Scriptures, and spiritual giftedness make each person in the church different from the others, but the Lord has assembled diverse churches so that members can help one another. In addition to the many means the Lord uses to help individual Christians grow in graciousness that we have considered in this book, every Christian should look around at the others within his or her church to seek examples of further ways to grow in graciousness. Your brothers and sisters in the church family also provide important corporate means of cultivating graciousness.

Spend Time with Gracious People

According to the Bible, there is a direct link between a person's closest companions and his or her behavior. Proverbs 13:20 says, "He who walks with wise men will be wise, but the companion of fools will be destroyed." Proverbs 22:24–25 says,

> Make no friendship with an angry man,
> And with a furious man do not go,
> Lest you learn his ways
> And set a snare for your soul.

The imitation dynamic revealed in the Bible goes both ways. On the one hand, as you spend time with wise or gracious people, you will literally become wiser and more gracious. If, on the other hand, you spend time with foolish or angry people known for explosive, rash outbursts, you will become a foolish, angry person who speaks recklessly as well. Without recognizing the process, your instincts and reactions become shaped by those who surround you. Some people naively assume that they are the exception to the Bible's rule, but everyone eventually discovers that they have become like the people with whom they have spent the most time.

The New Testament echoes the imitation dynamic throughout its pages. Paul plainly calls his readers to *imitate* or *mimic* his example as he follows Christ in both 1 Corinthians 11:1 and Philippians 4:9. In 2 Corinthians 8, he holds up the *example* of the sacrificial giving of the Macedonian churches for the Corinthians to follow. His readers are commended in 1 Thessalonians 1:5–8 for following Paul's *example* and for *being an example* themselves to other churches by joyfully receiving God's word amid persecution. To another church under threat of severe persecution came these words: "Remember those who rule over you, who have spoken the word of God to you, whose faith follow, considering the outcome of their conduct" (Heb. 13:7). A godly example so powerfully influences churches that the chief qualification for church leaders is godly character (see 1 Tim. 3:1–7; Titus 1:5–9). Peter notes that the primary means of an elder's leadership is his life example (1 Peter 5:1–4). Imitation is not just the sincerest form of flattery; God built the imitation dynamic into the fabric of human beings' souls.

Cultivating graciousness in community occurs as Christians spend time with gracious Christians. There are ways to do this even in an excessively busy Western culture. First, you should specifically identify people in your church marked by gentleness, loving interactions, and kind communication. You might ask, Whom would I want to be confronted by if I was wrong about an issue? Who seems the most patient with their children when they are acting up? Whom would my spiritual leaders recommend that I learn graciousness from? After you have identified some tenderhearted models, you should become intentional about spending time with them. If they are truly kindhearted, they will not be difficult to engage.

Then you should think about possible times to be together both inside and outside of church gatherings. Instead of rushing home to lunch after church, you should seek out the people you want to learn from. Even a few moments before and after church with some consistency add up to help you establish and build a friendship. Then you ought to invest time with these people outside of church meetings, such as a meal together in a home or restaurant, playing a sport or practicing a hobby together, or offering to work on a project with them. Any time you spend with gracious people will be beneficial to you as you grow in graciousness.

Becoming intentional during these meetings will amplify the benefits, as you seek to learn what makes the person gracious, observe the person's patterns of kindness unfolding in various circumstances, and even as you ask questions to learn about the thought patterns behind the sweetness of the person's words and deeds. The Bible states that everyone will imitate those they spend time with whether they are conscious of it or not, but those who want to become gracious ought to look for caring leaders to follow and seek to mimic them.

Ask for Help
Real friends help each other become more gracious while managing to remain friends. How can you know when to repent of an angry tone of voice? How can you identify a pattern of severity if you don't have anyone who loves you enough to point it out? While there are times a pugnacious person can figure out that he has been completely obnoxious, sometimes sarcasm or roughness is more subtle and makes

smaller displays. Without help from others to point out the problem, it is easy to miss. It is hard to point out faults to people—especially the sins that so clearly spring from a heart of pride. Growing in graciousness, however, requires true Christian friends who are willing to give one another wounding truths spoken in love, as Proverbs 27:6 says: "Faithful are the wounds of a friend, but the kisses of an enemy are deceitful."

Because of the challenges associated with giving and receiving correction, Christians who desire to become gracious should specifically charge their faithful friends to be on the lookout. You should ask your friends to take note of your words, tones, and facial expressions in your conversations. Then you should ask your friends to boldly point out any time that it seems like you are being less than gracious (the mere absence of harshness is not a high enough goal). Jerry Bridges suggested a series of pointed questions to ask friends who know the person best about ways they come across to others: "Are we dogmatic and opinionated, blunt and abrupt? Do we seek to intimidate or dominate others by the sheer force of our personality? Do people feel ill at ease in our presence because they think we are silently judging their weaknesses and correcting their faults? If any of these traits are characteristic of us, we must face them honestly and humbly."[1]

It requires humility to open up yourself even to a faithful friend, but if the seasoning of harshness consistently manifests itself in your communication, being gently exposed is exactly what you need. As has been noted, people cannot repent of

---

1. Jerry Bridges, *The Practice of Godliness* (Colorado Springs: NavPress, 1983), 228.

what they do not first see. Although you see some of your own faults, godly friends can often see more of them. Obviously no one wants the doctor to cut out only the big, obvious cancer while leaving all the smaller tumors in place, even if it means more pain for the patient and a longer recovery time.

In addition to asking for help in identifying occasions when your words or behavior is ungracious, you should ask your friend for specific advice or strategies to cultivate kindness in case the same situation recurs. General medicine can offer some help to a group of sick people, but a specific prescription given by someone who knows the details of the person's symptoms will prove to be a much more effective remedy. When Paul wanted to help the young church at Thessalonica, he wrote them a letter. While that was good, his deeper desire was to be personally present to adapt his counsel to their specific needs:

> But we, brethren, having been taken away from you for a short time in presence, not in heart, endeavored more eagerly to see your face with great desire.... Therefore, when we could no longer endure it, we thought it good to be left in Athens alone, and sent Timothy, our brother and minister of God, and our fellow laborer in the gospel of Christ, to establish you and encourage you concerning your faith, that no one should be shaken by these afflictions; for you yourselves know that we are appointed to this. (1 Thess. 2:17; 3:1–3)

Another benefit of having these types of difficult but good conversations with Christian friends about loving communication is that you and your friends who are involved can then pray for one another about the specific matters discussed.

While no person can change another person's heart, God can change any heart. Friends may plead on behalf of one another before the transforming God. Previously, we considered the personal discipline of begging for grace to become gracious. Here those good petitions are intensified by the intercessions of Christian friends. Whenever Paul desperately desired to be present with and help a needy group of Christians (like the Thessalonian church) but could not be, he could always pray for them.

Examples of Paul's prayers for the church abound in 1 Thessalonians:

> We give thanks to God always for you all, making mention of you in our prayers. (1:2)

> For this reason we also thank God without ceasing, because when you received the word of God which you heard from us, you welcomed it not as the word of men, but as it is in truth, the word of God, which also effectively works in you who believe. (2:13)

> For what thanks can we render to God for you, for all the joy with which we rejoice for your sake before our God, night and day praying exceedingly that we may see your face and perfect what is lacking in your faith? (3:9–10)

> Now may our God and Father Himself, and our Lord Jesus Christ, direct our way to you. And may the Lord make you increase and abound in love to one another and to all, just as we do to you, so that He may establish your hearts blameless in holiness before our God and Father at the coming of our Lord Jesus Christ with all His saints. (3:11–13)

When Christian friends make the effort to help you see your sin, you may not want to hear it; after all, these confrontations are rightly called "faithful wounds" (Prov. 27:6). As you long to cultivate graciousness, you should remind yourself of several things so that you become increasingly receptive to this painful but necessary reproof. First, you asked for it—literally. Second, the Bible is clear that fools refuse correction, but wise men and women accept it. One example of many is in Proverbs 9:7–9, which says:

> He who corrects a scoffer gets shame for himself,
> And he who rebukes a wicked man only harms himself.
> Do not correct a scoffer, lest he hate you;
> Rebuke a wise man, and he will love you.
> Give instruction to a wise man, and he will be still wiser;
> Teach a just man, and he will increase in learning.

In spite of how being reproved makes you feel emotionally, remembering this truth can strengthen your heart as you hear it. Finally, you should remind yourself that confrontation is the means the Lord has established to help people see and repent of their sin. You should thank God for sending you a faithful friend. You should thank your friend for his or her love and courage to be God's instrument to help you grow in graciousness.

Take the Initiative to Be Gracious in Group Contexts

Far too many Westerners think of church gatherings as spectator sports instead of participatory events. Consequently, within minutes of being dismissed, most of the people have dispersed. In healthy churches, however, members spend time with one another. The gathering of a local church ought to be a respite for God's people who are being barraged by the world the rest of the week. Church members ought to cherish these precious times together and use them to build relationships with others in the church family.

Because healthy churches are made up of mostly godly men and women seeking to reach out and minister to one another, church gatherings are wonderful occasions for Christians to practice being gracious. While it might seem artificial for you to intentionally manufacture a gracious comment to make to another person (as opposed to gentle sweetness naturally flowing from your grace-filled heart), sometimes discipline requires you to do what you know is right in spite of what is happening within your heart (1 Tim. 4:7–8). Even as a Christian, your heart will never cease to battle its remaining sin (Gal. 5:17). While it is important to depend on the Holy Spirit for spiritual progress, you must take responsibility and do what is right in spite of your feelings, trusting that the Holy Spirit will inspire your heart to follow (Phil. 2:12–13). You should intentionally seek to say kind words in kind ways to your fellow Christians when your church meets.

Sunday morning church gatherings often prove to be difficult times to have meaningful conversations. Not only do church members require discipline to be intentional about kind conversations but they also need discipline to create opportunities to talk with one another. You could schedule extra time before and especially after the service to interact with fellow church members. Certainly if the church offers less formal gatherings, such as Sunday school, a prayer meeting, or small group ministries, as you seek to have even more practice in graciousness you ought to attend those meetings as well.

As an intentional, disciplined pursuer of graciousness, instead of waiting for someone to speak to you, you should seek out someone with whom to start a conversation. It is not a bad idea to have a plan for the encounter in mind. You could use one of the means of cultivating graciousness already discussed to form the basis of your plan. Perhaps you want to try to listen better. You could initiate the conversation but then focus primarily on asking one or two questions and carefully listening to the answers. The next week, gracious helper words and phrases such as "it seems" and "from my perspective" may be your goal. Other times your aim could be expressing your gratitude or making an effort to communicate grace nonverbally. Engaging with fellow church members ought to be a major arena for your graciousness to be cultivated.

Establish a Reading Group

God's most spectacular natural creations are best admired from multiple perspectives. If you take the time and go to the expense of seeing the Grand Canyon or Niagara Falls, you should not be content to jump out of your vehicle at the first possible sighting, enjoy the view, take a few pictures, and then return home. Instead, you should move around to drink in the picture from different perspectives. Walking down a trail, driving to the next vista, crossing into New Mexico or Canada, and riding a donkey or boarding a boat provide opportunities for you to become even more amazed at and appreciative of these two masterpieces of God. Sermons and books that beautifully capture and apply the meaning of the Bible from different perspectives can be masterpieces for people's souls as well. The Lord raises up gifted men and women in every generation to teach and apply biblical truths to the issues of life. Reading their books or hearing the sermons of godly men can provide wonderful encouragement and instruction for growing Christians. Creating opportunities to discuss these books or sermons with others can multiply the benefits of the material, just as the multiple vantage points of a natural wonder multiply your amazement. Another way to cultivate graciousness in the context of the church community is to begin a reading group.[2]

Reading good books offers groups of Christians the chance to think carefully about a subject. The best Christian authors have studied the Scriptures, read the best literature on the matter, thought deeply about it, and carefully prepared their findings in books. Taking the time to read these books offers believers the opportunity to benefit directly from the labor of the author. But different people will respond differently to the same book. As a group of friends compares the contents of the book with what they know about the Bible's teaching and their own life experiences, a variety of insights will be sparked. Reading a book about God's providential superintending of the details of life, for example, might bring to someone's mind the book of Esther, in which God's powerful orchestration of the salvation of the Jews and the destruction of their enemies cannot be easily missed. The same book on divine providence, however, could be viewed differently by people

---

2. While the focus of this section is about discussing books, with the accessibility of sermons on the Internet, having a group discussion about sermons can be another fruitful application of this practice. Many small groups in churches discuss and apply the pastor's sermons. This same concept could work with Bible-based sermons preached elsewhere: a link to a sermon is sent through an e-mail, each group member downloads the sermon and listens to it, and then the group meets to discuss and apply the sermon's message.

who have had distinct personal experiences, like an adopted woman who discovered her biological parents in a way that could be explained only by God's hand, or like Joni Eareckson Tada, who had a tragic diving accident that left her paralyzed but found that God worked through her circumstances to create an international ministry to the disabled. As reading group participants offer their various perspectives, insights, knowledge of other Scriptures, and ideas for applications, the benefits of reading a good book are multiplied.

In addition to reading books specifically about gentleness, kindness, or godly communication, reading groups can cultivate graciousness by using other kinds of books. Even bad books can provide good help. If a reading group intentionally selected a popular book from a different theological point of view, for example, they could practice interacting with the book graciously. Instead of rolling their eyes, discussing only the worst points of the book, using biting sarcasm, insulting the author, judging his or her motives throughout the conversation, and stirring up one another's self-righteousness with hearty agreements and laughter, they could simply share their perspectives with Christian kindness. If the book is popular, others will probably be talking about it, and Christians often struggle for kind words to say when they find themselves unexpectedly in such conversations. Practicing graciousness with fellow church members can be helpful. While a good reading group will not overlook the errors of the book, they could seek to make positive points. Where is there common ground between the group and this book? Is there a burden this author is reacting to? Did the author expose any valid weaknesses in the theological position of the reading group? What are ways to help those who have been misled by this book discover its dangers without becoming offended by the people pointing them out?

A person who is kind when discussing a book that contains biblical errors is not affirming the errors. Like taking a practice test before the real exam, practicing kindness in the environment of a discerning reading group can prepare a person to be kind when he or she is unexpectedly asked his or her opinion of the book.

Books about God's grace to His children also can aid believers seeking to become more gracious. Group members celebrate God's greatness as they read books like J. I. Packer's *Knowing God*[3] or R. C. Sproul's *Chosen by God*,[4] and the lessons they learn will be reinforced in the hearts of the participants. Amazement at and love for the Lord intensify as Christians think deeply about the implications of God's grace. Discussing D. A. Carson's *Difficult Doctrine of the Love of God*,[5] John Stott's *Cross of Christ*,[6] or Jerry Bridges's *Transforming Grace*[7] can add to participants' knowledge and appreciation. As group members become more passionate about and grateful for God's grace to them, they will in turn become more gracious to those around them.

Just as spending time with gracious people cultivates graciousness, so also reading biographies of gracious people

---

3. J. I. Packer, *Knowing God* (Downers Grove, Ill.: IVP, 1993).

4. R. C. Sproul, *Chosen by God* (Wheaton, Ill.: Tyndale, 1994).

5. D. A. Carson, *The Difficult Doctrine of the Love of God* (Wheaton, Ill.: Crossway, 1999).

6. John R. W. Stott, *The Cross of Christ* (Downers Grove, Ill.: IVP, 2006).

7. Jerry Bridges, *Transforming Grace: Living Confidently in God's Unfailing Love* (Colorado Springs: NavPress, 2008).

provides examples for imitation. Theoretical kindness provides instruction, but lived kindness adds authenticity and tangibility to principles. Even Christians who are known for their sweet spirits have struggled to live consistently in a fallen world, and reading about and discussing their hard-learned lessons following sinful outbursts can be valuable to those facing similar ups and downs. Biographies provide both positive and negative examples. Reading and discussing biographies with other Christians helps us see details that we may have missed and provides us with more interpretive lenses to apply the lessons we learn to our own lives.

While there are many biographies that could provide wonderful discussions of graciousness lived out in real life, the following are good examples. The author of the famous hymn "Amazing Grace" was first spiritually blind before he could see. Biographies of John Newton show his journey from bold blasphemer to an Anglican pastor who was so kind that one time he canceled church just to be able to join the Baptists across town for their special speaker. Newton never got over God's grace to him, and that translated to gracious ministries in Olney, London, and all over the world through his books and letters.[8] Francis and Edith Schaeffer emerged from fundamentalism to reach out to questioning students in Switzerland in a

---

8. Jonathan Aitken, *John Newton: From Disgrace to Amazing Grace* (Wheaton, Ill.: Crossway, 2007). Aitken's biography is a wonderful place to get acquainted with John Newton. Newton's sweet letters are the place to go next; they provide examples of graciousness in action to people in a wide variety of situations. Evangelical Press has published a series called Bitesize Biographies that provides brief introductions to notable men and women in church history, including John Newton and other gracious believers mentioned here.

ministry called L'Abri. While he did not compromise his convictions about God's truth, Schaeffer was shaped by God into a winsome man who listened to and interacted with troubled young people's deepest spiritual questions and sought to give gracious, thoughtful answers from the Scriptures. All of this happened in a communal family context rather than a formal one, so that the spirit of hospitality marked the Schaeffers.[9]

Joni Eareckson Tada has suffered greatly ever since a diving accident in 1967, when she was seventeen, left her a quadriplegic in a wheelchair without the use of her hands. She recounts stories of wrestling with God and the peace that He provided through strong instruction about His sovereignty. Joni has grown in godly contentment, and the Lord has given her a tender heart to serve others with disabilities. Reading about these virtues in one who has suffered so much inspires graciousness in those who have suffered so little.[10]

Among theologians, Roger Nicole stands out as a man marked by graciousness. While some academicians seem to work in an ivory tower—researching, writing, and lecturing—Nicole understood his role as equipping his students for ministry and providing help for churches to fight against spiritual errors. He was unafraid to take strong stands on controversial

---

9. Colin Duriez, *Francis Schaeffer: An Authentic Life* (Wheaton, Ill.: Crossway, 2008). Duriez's biography describes the Schaeffers' journey in graciousness and in ministry. Francis and Edith wrote many books, letters, and articles characterized by speaking God's truth in love.

10. *Joni: An Unforgettable Story* (Grand Rapids: Zondervan, 2001) is the autobiography of her early years. Later, Tada wrote about her continuing challenges and ministry opportunities in *The God I Love: A Lifetime of Walking with Jesus* (Grand Rapids: Zondervan, 2003). Her other books provide a consistent model of God's sweetness through one of His daughters.

issues about the Bible and its teachings, even writing and debating against those he believed were wrong. But God gave Nicole the heart of a theological warrior tempered by the tenderness of Christian graciousness. Reading his story provides a marvelous model for Christians with great zeal for God's truth to speak that truth in love.[11]

For the arrow to hit its mark, the target must be visible. Good Christian books read in the company of faithful Christians can give a clear target of grace. Controversial books provide practice for interacting in gracious ways. Books about God and His grace fuel graciousness. Biographies of kind Christian men and women depict models of graciousness to follow.

Worship with the Church

The writer to the Hebrews exhorts, "Let us consider one another in order to stir up love and good works, not forsaking the assembling of ourselves together, as is the manner of some, but exhorting one another, and so much the more as you see the Day approaching" (10:24–25). A final way to cultivate graciousness within community is simply to heartily participate in the corporate means for growth that God has given churches. Each part of the church service can help you become more gentle and kind.

As a healthy church prays together and worships in song, the hearts of the people are lifted up as they talk to God and sing about His greatness and their smallness. People are grumpy, harsh, and calloused when they assume their own greatness and God's and everyone else's smallness. Worshiping

---

11. Bailey, *Speaking the Truth in Love*.

side by side with Christian brothers and sisters wonderfully reorients our perspective about the truly great One. Corporate prayers join the hearts and minds of a church family as together they praise and thank God for who He is and what He has done, confess their sins, and humbly seek Him with their petitions. Praying puts people in their proper place as creatures dependent on their Creator.

Another part of corporate worship is hearing the Scriptures both read and proclaimed. The preaching of the Word of God ought to have the same reorienting impact as the other parts of the worship service. Even if the Bible-based sermon is not directly about graciousness, it will always indirectly cultivate graciousness in hearers' hearts as God reveals Himself and His glorious ways through the Word. Biblical preaching acknowledges God's place and puts hearers in their places. These heart attitudes are foundational as you pursue godly communication with those around you.

The gospel is regularly proclaimed as the Word is faithfully preached, but the gospel is also portrayed as God's people participate in Communion. The Lord's Supper reminds believers about the bloody cross and the resurrection of the Lord Jesus Christ. As you humbly contemplate your own sins, for which Jesus was bearing God's wrath on the cross, you are filled with gratitude, joy, and hope. When you are struggling with the sins of your mouth (such as a lack of gracious words), you will discover both conviction and encouragement as the gospel is proclaimed in preaching or portrayed in Communion. All sins are extremely serious, but all the believer's sins are completely paid for. Raw conviction without gospel hope produces despair. Partaking of the Lord's Supper also puts you in your place—while you are desperate for God's mercy and grace, you are reminded that you are a recipient of God's mercy and grace through the work of Jesus Christ. The Lord's Supper also reminds you and the church that you are not alone. Surrounding you as you partake of the elements of Communion are your fellow believers who also desperately need God's grace and have freely received it from God.

Coming to church services faithfully cultivates graciousness as members seek to serve and encourage one another for the Lord's sake. Again, your gaze is moved from you and others as individuals and is fixed on the Lord and His people. This is the adjustment of humility. Humility is the most important heart attitude to develop as you pursue kind communication.

Conclusion

In the off-season, professional athletes who play team sports often work out alone, improving their skills for their role on the team. While those individual efforts usually pay dividends for the team, the greatest benefits for the team happen when all the individuals come together before the season for training camp. Intense group drills, meetings, and workouts under expert coaches and trainers help each team member work in harmony with the others. The result will be better than any individual could accomplish on his or her own. In the same way, God blesses you as you take responsibility to grow and change on your own, but your fruitfulness will multiply as you work on changing side by side with your brothers and sisters in the body of Christ.

Chapter 10

The Gospel and Graciousness

The eighteenth-century slave trader turned gracious pastor John Newton once wrote a letter to a friend who was contending for God's truth, which was later published with the title "On Controversy."[1] The old sea captain, who referred to himself as a wretch saved by God's amazing grace, highly esteemed his friend's zeal for God's truth. He declared, "It seems a laudable service to defend the faith once delivered to the saints; we are commanded to contend earnestly for it, and to convince gainsayers. If ever such defences were seasonable and expedient, they appear to be so in our day, when errors abound on all sides, and every truth of the Gospel is either directly denied, or grossly misrepresented."[2]

Newton was convinced that earnestly declaring God's truth was laudable, but he joined his encouragement with strong warnings: "If our zeal is embittered by expressions of anger, invective, or scorn, we may think we are doing service to the cause of truth, when in reality we shall only bring it

---

1. John Newton, "On Controversy," in *Works of John Newton* (Edinburgh: Banner of Truth Trust, 1985), 1:268.
2. Newton, "On Controversy," 273.

into discredit."[3] He warned that "self-righteousness can feed upon doctrines, as well as upon works; and a man may have the heart of a Pharisee, while his head is stored with orthodox notions of the unworthiness of the creature and the riches of free grace."[4]

Newton called on his reader, when taking a stand for the Scriptures, to pray for his own heart and for the one with whom he would be communicating, to have the Lord's compassion for his adversary and to remember that it is always God who changes hearts. He counseled his friend that although defending God's truth is honorable, it is also spiritually dangerous: "What will it profit a man if he gains his cause, and silences his adversary, if at the same time he loses that humble, tender frame of spirit in which the Lord delights, and to which the promise of his presence is made!"[5] Newton's concern for the vital combination of zeal for God's truth and Christlike tenderness is as relevant today as when he penned his letter.

While the Spirit of God faithfully creates the kind of gentle character within the hearts of true believers in Christ that the Word of God requires, believers are also responsible to use every means available to cultivate the heart attitudes that lead to consistently gracious interactions with others. As you grow in your knowledge and love for God's truth, you must fight your pride against using God's truth to club those around you. As the Lord Jesus has been so kind, patient, and gracious to you, those marks must melt your heart. When

---

3. Newton, "On Controversy," 271.
4. Newton, "On Controversy," 272.
5. Newton, "On Controversy," 273.

you read about the various ways that you could cultivate more graciousness, did the Holy Spirit convict you of specific areas of remaining harshness? Even though this is humbling, it is more proof of the Lord's love for you. If He didn't care about you, He wouldn't continue to deliver you from your former gruff ways. He kindly convicts; He kindly disciplines; He kindly crushed His Son to die for all your failures to be kind (Isa. 53:6–7; Heb. 12:6).

As your heart becomes softened by His transforming grace, you should be motivated to do what it takes, with the Spirit's help, to communicate that same grace to everyone around you. Many means of cultivating graciousness have been presented in this book, beginning with the Bible's commands for Christians to be gracious. You have seen how the examples of the Lord Jesus and the apostle Paul painted portraits of graciousness, while the case of the church at Ephesus illustrated the spiritual danger of zeal for truth apart from love. We have also identified many practical ways to nurture graciousness individually and in community.

When Christians within a church make progress in practicing biblical graciousness, there are many benefits. When you deal with one another, you will grow stronger as you speak God's truth in love. The context for Paul's command to speak the truth in love is the mutual ministry of one member to another, which produced spiritual maturity of the parts, which results in the maturity of the whole. Paul summarizes the process and the outcome: "But, speaking the truth in love, [you] may grow up in all things into Him who is the head—Christ—from whom the whole body, joined and knit together by what every joint supplies, according to the effective working by which every part does its share, causes growth of the body for the edifying of itself in love" (Eph. 4:15–16). Gracious words from God, spoken in gracious ways by God's people, provide comfort, encouragement, exhortation, conviction, instruction, training, hope, wisdom for decisions, counsel, and discernment for His people to live in His world. As God's Word is profitable for comprehensive Christian maturity (2 Tim. 3:16–17), gracious communication of that Word to one another ought to be a hallmark of God's people's interactions.

Churches filled with graciousness and truth will be well suited to interact in a helpful way with other churches. The book of Acts and the letters of the New Testament give several examples of churches working together. Local churches coordinated offerings of money to supply the needs of the poor church in Jerusalem (2 Cor. 8:16–24), gathered to work on doctrine related to the gospel and the Gentiles (Acts 15), and gave money to help further the work of the gospel (Phil. 4:15; 3 John 5–8). As individual believers are strengthened to spiritual maturity through kind interactions with other believers, so also entire churches are aided by gracious cooperative efforts with sister churches to honor God and accomplish His work together.

A church that reaches out to its community in love often creates a platform for Christians to proclaim the gospel. The Lord Jesus described love as the distinctive mark of His followers: "A new commandment I give to you, that you love one another; as I have loved you, that you also love one another. By this all will know that you are My disciples, if you have love for one another" (John 13:34–35). In His Sermon on the Mount, Jesus taught that good works which express Christian love point the observers to God: "Let your light so shine before men, that they may see your good works and glorify your Father in heaven" (Matt. 5:16). Loving heart attitudes produce not only good works but also speech seasoned with grace. Such distinct "salty" living and speaking creates gospel opportunities for churches. Thus, the apostle Paul instructed, "Walk in wisdom toward those who are outside, redeeming the time. Let your speech always be with grace, seasoned with salt, that you may know how you ought to answer each one" (Col. 4:5–6). A gracious church will impact a community.

John Newton concluded his letter "On Controversy" with a wonderful charge and benediction that Christians of all ages would do well to follow: "Go forth, therefore, in the name and strength of the Lord of Hosts, speaking the truth in love; and may he give you a witness in many hearts, that you are taught of God, and favoured with the unction of his Holy Spirit."[6]

---

6. Newton, "On Controversy," 274.